Praise for *The Bright Way*

"Drawing from many traditions, *The Bright Way* offers a frie[...] for reconnecting with one's own artistic voice, no matter ho[...] [...] covering the profound joy of the creative process can be life-changing — utterly transformative — and lots of fun, especially with Diana Rowan as your guide."
— Sam Bennett, author of *Get It Done* and *Start Right Where You Are*

"Diana Rowan's beautiful book will be an invaluable guide and inspiration for anyone who has felt exiled from their creative self. There are depth and wisdom here; the author's five steps offer a powerful yet accessible and practical process that will help even the most creatively blocked of us share our gifts joyfully and confidently with the world. *The Bright Way* shines; in its pages, creativity becomes a magical, transformative, and healing practice that enriches both self and community."
— Philip Carr-Gomm, author of
Lessons in Magic and *Empower Your Life with Sophrology*

"Drawing on the riches of the world's wisdom traditions and her own personal experience, Diana Rowan invites the reader on a journey to the creative spark that is the birthright of every human being. Filled with inventive exercises and compassionate encouragement, *The Bright Way* offers people from all walks of life a practical road map to the creative life."
— Gail Needleman, cocreator of the online American Folk Song Collection
(http://kodaly.hnu.edu)

"This is that rarest of things, the self-help book that will actually help! And for the most abstract and elusive of pursuits, creativity. Every creative person knows the paralysis of performance anxiety or being blocked — including the author, who so revealingly shares that experience, and maps a beautiful way out of it."
— Bob Guccione Jr., editor and publisher of *WONDERLUST*

"This illuminated manuscript presents a beautiful path to overcoming blocks and anxiety so that you can do what matters most: live your purpose, give your gifts, and connect with others."
— Kaia Alexander (a.k.a. K. Hollan Van Zandt), award-winning
author of *Written in the Ashes*

"If you've been feeling stagnant in any aspect of your life, *The Bright Way* will guide you to a path of illumination and newfound creativity. Diana Rowan paints in words a clear understanding of how to access a well of peace and worthiness."

— Joanna Garzilli, award-winning author of *Big Miracles*

"Artist and author Diana Rowan has given us a gift. She grounds lofty philosophies and themes in practical language and lessons, with detailed guidance on discovering, exercising, sharing, and rejoicing in each person's creative self....A virtuoso performance."

— Patrice Adcroft, former editor in chief of *Seventeen* magazine and author of *Every Day Doughnuts* and *Mother, Father, Me*

"If you have ever felt stuck or unsure about sharing your creativity with the world, please read Diana Rowan's personal story of recovery and how she harnessed her fears by learning to share from her heart. If you have any inkling of doubt about sharing your creative gifts with the world, *The Bright Way* will guide you in fulfilling your creative purpose."

— Cary Broussard, author of *From Cinderella to CEO* and CEO of Broussard Global Communications

"A powerful tool for all on the creative path, *The Bright Way* guides us to reconnect with our innate creative selves. Diana Rowan is a wise and loving mentor on this journey. She distills the ancient intuitive art of creativity into a thorough, practical, and clear pathway for us all."

— Alice Giles, world-renowned harpist

"The extraordinary Irish-born musician Diana Rowan provides a much-needed window into the creative process and spirit within each of us."

— Sam Barry, author of *How to Play the Harmonica and Other Life Lessons*

The Bright Way

The Bright Way

Five Steps to Freeing the Creative Within

Diana Rowan

Illustrations by Vladimir Baltić

New World Library
Novato, California

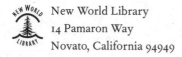 New World Library
14 Pamaron Way
Novato, California 94949

Illustrations by Vladimir Baltić
Text design by Tona Pearce Myers

Library of Congress Cataloging-in-Publication Data

Names: Rowan, Diana, date, author.
Title: The bright way : five steps to freeing the creative within / Diana Rowan ; illustrations by Vladimir Baltić.
Description: Novato, California : New World Library, [2020] | Includes bibliographical references. | Summary: "A musician and teacher gives aspiring artists, writers, and musicians practical techniques to overcome creative blocks and performance anxiety. The book includes skill-building exercises, meditations, and affirmations to increase confidence and creativity."--Provided by publisher.
Identifiers: LCCN 2019049213 (print) | LCCN 2019049214 (ebook) | ISBN 9781608686445 (paperback) | ISBN 9781608686452 (epub)
Subjects: LCSH: Creative ability.
Classification: LCC BF408 .R7245 2020 (print) | LCC BF408 (ebook) | DDC 153.3/5--dc23
LC record available at https://lccn.loc.gov/2019049213
LC ebook record available at https://lccn.loc.gov/2019049214

First printing, March 2020
ISBN 978-1-60868-644-5
Ebook ISBN 978-1-60868-645-2
Printed in Canada on 100% postconsumer-waste recycled paper

 New World Library is proud to be a Gold Certified Environmentally Responsible Publisher. Publisher certification awarded by Green Press Initiative.

10   9   8   7   6   5   4   3   2   1

I see the eternal flame inside you:
You were born with this bright light.
May our journey unveil your true radiance,
Blazing your joy from the inside out,
Lighting up the lives of all around you,
Shining your Bright Knowledge down through the ages to come.
You are stronger than you know:
Throw down your shields, and declare yourself boldly.
Together let's illuminate your way
Back to your true self, Bright One.
Welcome home.

Contents

Part Three: Homecoming

PART ONE

Invitation and Initiation

As Above,
So Below

The concert finishes, the house lights blaze, and applause rings out. I take a bow happily and bound off the stage to meet my audience. And it happens, as always; among the people surrounding me, several approach with a particular shyness I've come to recognize. They hail from all walks of life, yet they share a deeply hidden desire. Sometimes they know my dramatic story of severe performance anxiety and how I finally managed to recover from it. Others know me only as a performer, composer, writer, and teacher and generously assume that I've always had confidence and motivation. Either way, there are two things they probably don't know: the vast potential they hold inside themselves, and how much their story is my story.

Rewind three decades. I remember one concert in particular, a showcase of the top student pianists. When I was fifteen, my diplomat family moved to Baghdad while I attended high school in nearby Cyprus. The concert, which took place during my second year there, was a special occasion for me because my father was present. I was the only representative of my teacher's studio that evening, so I wanted to make my piano teacher, Kleri, proud. But I was at the height of self-consciousness; my body had betrayed me in a most awkward phase of frizzy hair, braces, and acne. Climbing the stairs to the stage, I felt dumpy, absurd, and fragmented into a thousand shards of stress. Ice-cold nervous sweat trickled down my back and spiked out under my arms as I confronted the looming beast of a piano.

The audience waited silently. I thought about my father and my teacher sitting there in the shadows, expectantly. The room became a vacuum. My ears dialed the silence up to a roar. I launched into Poulenc's Nocturne no. 1 — only to be catapulted out within three bars.

The piano keys — keys that had been my daily companions for almost a decade — mocked me as they danced, rearranging themselves before my eyes. I couldn't regain a handhold in the music. Clutching at the song, I hoped my fingers would somehow remember what to do on their own. They betrayed me, too, with a grotesque parody of the song I thought I knew so well clanging in my ears. Titters arose from some boys in my class, the same ones who bullied me about my appearance every day. I was mortified that my father had come all the way from Baghdad to witness this fiasco. I felt sure he was ashamed that I was his daughter, especially given that my mother is beautiful and accomplished. I was a total disappointment.

Mercilessly I threw myself in again. This time I made even less headway. My stomach twisted in the knowledge that my teacher was watching all this. She could only feel that I was letting her down in the most public way possible. I dreaded damaging our close relationship. Cringing at the evidence left behind, having sweat all over the keyboard and the piano bench, I fled the stage as quickly as possible. The hall filled with outright laughter from my tormentors and appalled silence from everyone else.

Today people can't believe I was ever like this. Yet it was in this fiery crucible of suffering that I eventually came to understand our deepest reasons for creating and, further, why our creativity *must* be given voice. If I hadn't gone through this degree of pain, feeling as if my very validity as a human being was on endless trial, I wouldn't have gone the distance it took to uncover the lessons you hold in your hands today. Necessity is the mother of invention, and I needed to escape my personal hell. The mother of invention gifted me generously, ultimately leading me to transform the prison of my fear into the freedom of love. Yes, it was arduous work (and still is sometimes). Reasonably so: it is the Great Work that we all undertake to encounter our true selves.

Knowing what I know now fires me up with enthusiasm to share this truth: *there is a brighter way*. What you seek, you *will* find. I want to impart this to all who approach me about their creative issues and anxieties: there *are* answers to your suffering and your longing. The Bright Way is one of those answers.

My fellow creative seekers reach out to me in many ways: anonymously online, privately via email, safely within my teaching groups and online conferences, through chance encounters in cafés. They believe they struggle alone. Not so: their hidden desires mirror one another's with striking faithfulness. I'm honored to be privy to their secret hopes and fears. They yearn to find more meaning in what they do and who they are. These seekers long to be part of a bigger picture, to feel they have something valuable to offer. To experience more joy. To live in flow and connection. To believe there is time and space for any of these things.

Urgency marks their voices. These are not mere wants. They are true needs.

Since these are such powerful needs, why do we hesitate to share our struggles? Tragically, we often blame ourselves for having these needs. We feel ashamed that our deepest desires have become mysteries to us. We mourn the fading of our once-bright dreams. We feel trapped, like passive watchers of our own lives. Perhaps these feelings have been haunting you, too? If so, take heart: you're not alone, and even more important, it doesn't have to be this way.

> *Like billowing clouds, like the incessant gurgle of the brook,*
> *the longing of the spirit can never be stilled.*

— St. Hildegard of Bingen, twelfth-century mystic, musician, and healer

I salute all brave seekers. I salute you. Giving voice to your frustration can be painful and scary. Yet it's a crucial first step toward fulfilling yourself creatively. Taking a stand for your desires (even if only in private) automatically directs you toward change, as my harp student Edela explains so well: "Just listening to music isn't enough for me. It is as senseless as trying to be nourished by a beautiful photograph of food rather than having food before me." You'll meet Edela again soon.

The popular professor tortured by Impostor Syndrome so extreme that he literally pulls his hair out; the pianist who has played for twenty years, though no one, not even her parents, has heard her because of her performance anxiety; the writer who has lost faith that creativity even matters in this crazy world; the successful businessperson who is terrified he will look foolish by indulging his longing to improvise; the dedicated amateur artist who suspects she doesn't really "have it" and never will; the jaded professional artist who is loath to admit he has tired of his craft; the busy mother who fears she has traded her creativity for child-rearing. Despite how different these people are, their core story is the same: *they feel a wrenching disconnection from what they rightly believe are their true selves.*

I remember these feelings myself. Simply recalling those grim days activates the horrible pull of that void. The words of Wendolyn Bird, founder of an outdoor preschool, storyteller, and harpist, echo exactly where I once was: "I've stopped performing due to anxiety. I won't play in front of people, even though I actually love to do so. I feel sad, frustrated, angry, and alone for not being able to just play freely and when I wish to. It stops my practice and/or alters it so that I never learn anything or advance to the point of being able to play even with friends."

Although the stories I've shared so far focus mainly on performance anxiety, the lessons this plight has taught me hold true for all creative endeavors. Performance anxiety is an extreme manifestation of the fears we all hold inside us when it comes to engaging and sharing our creativity. As such, it's a powerful lens through which to examine what it takes to reclaim your creativity for life.

It's hard to believe just how common the suffering caused by disconnection from our creativity is. But I've seen it with my own eyes. Repeatedly, and over many years. I thought my problems were unique until I started teaching music and collaborating full-time with other creative people from around the world. I worked with everyone from beginners to seasoned pros of all ages and backgrounds, and clouds of anxiety, burnout, frustration, and grief haunted us all. People three decades older than I became as vulnerable as little children, crying as they finally exposed their lost hopes and dreams in the privacy of my studio.

The stakes felt hair-raisingly high. The deepest questions of what makes life worth living were being presented to me. Simply living and growing older didn't answer those questions. As a child, in awe of the adults surrounding me, I always assumed that somehow we'd all just figure things out over time. Now I know how many of those adults must have really felt — and many still feel — inside.

It was a lot to take in and hold. What could I do about it? Even though it was a relief not to be alone in my own struggle with performance anxiety, watching others suffer through it was torture. As the teacher, I felt duty bound to dredge up some sort of solution. But what? For a long time, I was barely one step ahead on the outside and often felt a league behind on the inside.

This struggle isn't just about you and me. It's about all of us. Even those who appear to live creative and successful lives on the outside often feel like frauds on the inside. This sense of disconnection casts a dreadful spell over our world. The consequences? Increased anxiety, depression, frustration, lack of motivation, loneliness, creeping hopelessness about our capabilities and even our futures as work options shrivel and mortality rates rise. This malaise infects our spirits, our families, our communities. The pain is real.

Astonishingly, given the scope of this scourge, an antidote does exist. It has for a long time, and it is hidden in plain sight. It is an approach, a way of life, that is simple and can be applied to every creative activity you engage in. It is a path that returns you to your true self, resurrecting your innate joy, honing your complementary powers of skill and intuition, and giving you the courage to reclaim your purpose, your creativity, and your destiny.

Whether you believe that life has inherent meaning or that the whole of existence is a preposterous accident, *this way still holds true*. From the spiritual teachings of Plato, Buddha, Jesus, and St. Catherine of Siena to diverse world belief systems, all the way to the nihilism of Nietzsche, the existentialism of Camus, and the "unselfing" of Irish philosopher Iris Murdoch, the conclusion has been the same: the meaning of life is to connect with life.

> The meaning of life is to connect with life.

And what is one of the surest and most beautiful ways to connect with life? In a word, it is to *engage your creativity*.

I'm willing to make this claim because I've experienced it

time and time again. And this is why I developed the Five Step Bright Way System: to give you (and myself!) a way to reignite and follow through on your magnificent creativity, starting today.

I have many favorite stories of the rewards gained from living this philosophy, so let me highlight just a few: the photographer rejecting plans to attend law school and transforming a jaded perspective of their work as being "just a cash register" into an unprecedented devotion to cultivating artistic community. The accomplished veteran musician catapulting herself to an inspired level of artistry after twenty years of uneventful practice. Our Edela, a retired school principal who fulfilled her lifelong dream of taking up the harp and performed in public regularly within a year of working with me, despite a seven-decade-long history of performance anxiety.

And Wendolyn, whom you met a few pages back at the height of her frustration? She reports on performing at her daughter's wedding, an event of huge import and pressure for her: "An exuberantly joyful day for me today! After forty-five years of playing the harp and practicing in a way that no longer serves me, I found *my* own rhythm and joy. My connection to the harp has greater depth now, and I found an entryway into allowing myself to *be* with what was deeply congruent with the essence of me in the moment. I am grateful to have this place to share my joy. Thank you to any who have received this moment with me."

BRIGHT WAY ACTIVITY
What Brought You Here?

Throughout this book you'll find Bright Way Activities marking your way like beacons of light. For your initiatory activity, take a few minutes to consider where you are right now. What brought you to this book? What fears and stressors are holding you back from living creatively? Write down your reflections. Let's get a baseline of where you are as we prepare to walk this path together. Know that change can happen anytime, anyplace, at any age. Let's make it happen for you.

As Above, So Below:
The Power of Changing Your Mindset

Before we start walking the Bright Way, I must share an essential truth with you. I have learned from decades of teaching and creating that *mindset is everything*. By *mindset*, I mean what you believe body-mind-spirit about yourself and about what's possible for you.

Simply put, if you believe you can do something, you can. If you don't believe you can do something, you can't. If you place limitations of any sort on yourself, I have to tell you, they *will* play out. While this might sound scary, the opposite is also true: *if you adopt a mindset of possibility, growth, and unlimited potential, your life will blossom in response.* This is the mindset I invite you to adopt on our path.

As Above, So Below; the Bright Way will ask you to change your mindset on many things — always from a compassionate place of love, growth, and connection — so that your life reflects your innermost dreams. You'll have the opportunity to let go of old ways of thinking and being that have held back your creativity — until now.

If our process begins to feel shocking or brings up fear, remember this: the Bright Way stands for life affirmation of the highest order: affirmation of *your* life. Furthermore, you are not alone on this path. I am here with you, along with the many other Bright Way practitioners spanning the globe, all in a fellowship of life celebration. We are excited you are here!

Changing your mindset is exhilarating, liberating, and, yes, rigorous. This is why part 1 of this book is called "Invitation and Initiation." It prepares you to take the Five Bright Way Steps explored in part 2 by gently initiating you into the philosophy first. I hope you receive this invitation wholeheartedly and voluntarily. *You are in charge on this path*. There are no gatekeepers on the Bright Way, no bosses; it is your courage that urges you on. Propelled by your courage, you'll self-initiate into the great secrets of creativity that have been known throughout the ages. You are here because you heeded the call.

Let's begin your initiation with one of the most important Bright Way principles: creativity is *connection*.

Creativity Is Connection

When you create, you connect. As you engage with your chosen activity, you become one with it. We've learned from physics that when we interact with something, we change it. This interaction is *connection made manifest*, sparked by your direct engagement.

When we make our mark on something through creative engagement, we see our true selves reflected back. This mirroring gives us a deep sense of belonging and meaning. Our existence is affirmed. *We know that we matter.* Our confidence is restored. Your entry point to this way of life? It's what you already possess: your creativity.

This is why creativity matters in and of itself: it is a reflection of you that literally makes you feel more, well, *you*. It confirms your place in the world. It acknowledges your dignity and your right to exist — and everyone else's — simply because you're alive. Creativity reminds you that you are worthy in and of yourself. Therefore, *it is the act of being creative that matters most, not the products of your creativity, because creativity has no agenda beyond life affirmation through connection.*

All tangible side effects such as glorious works of art, inspiring performances, and brilliant innovations are magnificent blessings and encouragements. Yet they all spring from same source: life affirmation. Keep focused on this primary matter, this first principle, and your creative process will flourish.

Disconnection is one of the most terrifying sensations we experience as human beings. Think of the immediate and intense distress babies feel when separated from their parents. When we get disconnected, we feel horribly unsafe. Disconnection doesn't have to be dramatic to have an impact. Simply feeling set apart from others in everyday life can trigger extreme anxiety and depression. Disconnection from our true selves is perhaps the most frightening of all when, severed from source energy itself, we wonder if life has any meaning.

> Your entry point to this way of life? It's what you already possess: your creativity.

> Creativity has no agenda beyond life affirmation through connection.

Our survival as human beings depends on being connected. The reality is, most of us wouldn't last more than a few days alone in the forest. Surviving, let alone thriving, demands creativity. Humans are not endowed with protective fangs or formidable physical strength. We don't even run very fast relative to other creatures! Our superpower is our spectacular creativity. It's our adaptability rather than our strength or intellect alone that has allowed us to survive. Creativity is by its nature ever changing. Adapting to the present situation, creativity then elaborates on it, bringing forth ever more vital expressions of life force. The circle of life turns: creativity affirming life, life sparking creativity.

Our creativity has protected humanity through millennia of radical change. Creativity urged us to evolve. If we want to keep evolving — if we want to further our individual and collective life force — we must stay creative. All this points to creativity's grandest message: life is worth affirming and amplifying, because it is the energy of connection — love — made manifest.

Many types of therapy aim to reconnect us to the world, to ourselves, to our source. Astounding breakthroughs can happen when we reestablish the connections in our lives, as neuroscientist Candace Pert affirms: "Love is an integrator and a healer, but you have to do the work to love yourself, and you can start by loving others. That's the core of human health."

Life is worth affirming and amplifying, because it is the energy of connection — love — made manifest.

I had a stunning revelation during deep meditation when I suddenly perceived how everything is interconnected. A wave of relief washed over me, and my life changed forever. While this may sound incredible, my direct experience tells me that when connection is restored, we are safe again. Fear fades, love takes center stage, and we become ourselves once more.

This illumination has stayed with me, and those close to me have remarked that I have been more myself since then. The change can become permanent because once you receive this knowledge, you can't un-know it. This is why your creativity, your direct engagement with life, is so important: it reconnects you, for life. I want this for you.

Engaging your innate creativity is one of the quickest, safest, most available, satisfying, and positive ways to do this. As Above, So Below: reclaim your creativity, reclaim your life. On the Bright Way, it is an article of faith that you aren't broken. The Bright Way doesn't try to "fix" you. Rather, it reminds you of who you truly are. By being creative, by actively engaging in your life, you *will* remember who you are. Welcome to the magnificence of your true self.

Welcome home.

> Engaging your innate creativity is one of the quickest, safest, most available, satisfying, and positive ways to restore your connection to yourself and to the world at large.

Your Story
Is My Story

The creative quest is one of the most thrilling journeys we can take. Yet it can also feel overwhelming at the outset. I understand this because I lost touch with my own creativity for decades.

Adrift starting around the age of ten, I only regained my bearings in my early thirties. Despite years of musical study and accomplishments, I felt as if I was clawing around in darkness for a thread of security. Those nightmarish fears performers have? You've already seen that I endured them in public: suffering major memory lapses onstage, throwing up before performances, feeling humiliated as I shook like a leaf in front of hundreds of people, running offstage, refusing to go onstage — among other horrors. Performance anxiety is one of the most traumatic and seemingly mysterious problems artists endure. This fear isn't just theoretical; it was physically, emotionally, and spiritually crushing.

Years of teaching confirm for me that our stories reflect one another's. My guess is that you already relate to much of what I've shared. Allow me to continue weaving our stories together so that you can walk this path of transformation with me.

How did I find myself in such a predicament in the first place? My creative journey started optimistically, as many journeys do. I took up piano at age eight. My delight in playing, practicing, and generally being around the piano as much as possible made it clear right away that I would become a professional musician. Perhaps you have joyful early memories of creative encounters, too? As I entered the magical world of music, everything became hyper-real for me. Regular life seemed less vivid, less true, while the musical world bathed me in something golden, bright, eternal. I was home.

It didn't take long for this reverie to fade. Yes, I was following my bliss, but the ride got rough, and fast. The pressure of exams, recitals, and competitions crushed the joy out of everything. I started avoiding practice, fearing lessons, agonizing over whether I had the exceptional talent to be a professional musician. Maybe you recognize some of these feelings?

Nonetheless, I persevered. I loved music; surely that was a sign that I'd been chosen as gifted? How impossibly cruel life would be if that were not so! But the fears made me doubt my abilities. Were my fears warning me that I didn't "have it"?

I hoped the fears would fade with time, but they grew worse. The more I accomplished, the higher the stakes became. The battle was relentless. My performance anxiety infected all areas of my life. My short fuse blew small disagreements into major showdowns. I took offense at even the most innocent comments and interactions. I lost trust in my body's ability to heal itself, became deaf to its signals, and even began to see it as my enemy. In all areas I tortured myself about the ever-present prospect of making public and private mistakes. If any of this sounds familiar to you, I send you a beam of love to fuel your courage going forward.

Casting about for a lifeline, I grappled for that treasure trove of knowledge others seemed to possess. Those in-crowd people who create and perform with joy — why was I so different from them? I needed to exit this vortex, and fast.

Performances cropped up regularly. The next exam was always around the corner. And, ironically, the intensity was only going to increase as I got more accomplished. I needed to show up with confidence and inspiration, not as the pathetic figure of weakness I embodied. My ears rang and my eyes watered. I went from vortex to black hole, endlessly craving and swallowing positive feedback, which vaporized instantly. There was no relief. The pressure kept mounting. Nothing made sense. I felt the greatest of fears: that I was alone.

Finally, during my second semester as a music major at the university, I couldn't bear it any longer. I quit music cold. I was only eighteen years old and believed the life I had hoped for was already over.

Retreat

My self-imposed exile from music lasted four long years. I worked in the health field, mostly in social welfare and psychology settings, and studied classics, a favorite subject for me in high school. Among the places I worked was a battered women's shelter and hotline; the front desk of the Berkeley Free Clinic, which provides healthcare to the homeless; and a halfway house. As I witnessed people suffering the extremes of domestic violence, poverty, addiction, and ill health, I noticed a common thread connecting them all.

They all wanted to experience joy and belonging, just like everyone else. Whatever their particular circumstances, in all cases their personal power had been obliterated. How could they reclaim that power? I didn't have an answer then. But these fellow travelers in life told me that finding at least one answer was a quest I couldn't refuse. They directed me to my starting point: the knowledge that reclaiming your power is essential to human fulfillment. Yet I remained mystified about how to take on what seemed an outlandishly large mission.

Still separated from my music making, whenever I'd hear even so much as piano Muzak in the elevator, I'd burst into tears, stabbed by the pain of loss. If you are living with this kind of pain right now, I hold you in my heart. Your pain is real, and you need to listen to it. Your pain is not your enemy; it is pointing you toward a better way, a better life.

Looking back, I see as clear as day that I was disconnected from my true self and, as an inevitable consequence, disconnected from my power and creativity. How did I discover all this on my own? I didn't! Despite having believed I was alone in my struggle, it turns out that clues and quiet assistance had been present all along.

Your pain is not your enemy; it is pointing you toward a better way, a better life.

Enter the Allies

Take heart. I discovered that my allies had been gathering around me my entire life, and I've found this to be true for almost everyone. *You have far more support eagerly waiting in the wings than you know.* We'll be finding out who and what your supports are soon. Who and what were my allies?

My parents were still college students when I was born. I enjoyed being the novelty only child among the young, wild Dublin intellectuals of the '70s. My father became a diplomat for the Irish government when I was three, giving me the opportunity to grow up all over the world, moving countries every four years or so. I got firsthand experience of the wondrous variety of ways that cultures encourage and interpret human creativity.

You have far more support eagerly waiting in the wings than you know.

This alliance of cultures illuminated new possibilities for me, which I will share with you throughout our journey together. As my creative journey matured, I learned how to incorporate these new perspectives. For example, by moving to California I encountered African music masters who introduced me to a playful freedom where "wrong" notes are understood simply as what chose to show up at that moment. Touring with bansuri maestro Deepak Ram, I witnessed the unabashedly spiritual foundation of Indian music, where surrender to the divine is second nature. Living in Cyprus and Iraq and traveling all over the Middle East, I participated in the ecstatic communing of that region's music, where the self, the ego, is not the focus. These were the oases I strung together to form a new continent of creativity. Eventually these diverse influences coalesced into an ethos I could live by.

Each of these influences is mighty in its own right; together, they form a lifeline guiding me through today's labyrinthine world.

My most pointed ally intervention came from my mother. At twenty-one, I was three years into my music-abandonment period. I met Phyllis — I've always called my mum by her first name; my parents' college friends addressed her that way, which I copied before she realized what was happening — for an afternoon drink. We convened at the prophetically named Orbit Room in San Francisco. At the crossroads of five busy streets and encased in massive glass windows, the place feels like you're floating in space and time. And that's where I was, lost in space, tethered to the world only by an as-yet-unseen star.

Phyllis got to the point: "What happened to you and music? It used to be everything to you."

A couple of glasses of wine in, I began to weep. Lost years weighed on me, failure leered, desire rose in me, only to be dashed: "I'm too old to go back." Phyllis looked at me incredulously. In my mind, you needed to have won a piano competition by my age to even imagine having a professional career. That was out of the question, with my shattered nerves. Case closed.

Quietly, Phyllis said, "You're only too old if you think you're too old."

I don't know why this got through to me, but something clicked right there and then. My limited thinking suddenly felt like chains I had locked on myself. The contradiction was untenable: here I was trying to help other people — some of them old enough to be my grandparents — to reclaim their power while privately destroying my own. I surrendered. The fact was, as crazy as it sounded, I was *choosing* this path of misery. I confessed to myself that my perception was out of whack more than any degree of accomplishment or "talent." If I changed my mindset, which thankfully I had seen other brave souls do, it could change my experience...and changing my experience would change *everything*! Could I have another chance at my life?

> You're only too old if you think you're too old.

As I gained a tentative toehold back in the music world, the *how* of which I'll share with you later, I didn't abandon my work in shelters and continued on as a volunteer. I remember teaching piano to a gentleman in the halfway house in San

Francisco's notorious Tenderloin district. Despite struggling desperately with addiction, when he picked out his bare-bones blues during lessons on that big old donated Hammond organ, he lit up, fueled by his own steam for the first time in a long time. The energy in the room changed palpably as his true power sparked to life. I remember a woman who had suffered major depression for forty years telling me with amazement that playing harp was more effective than any of the dozens of strong medications she'd relied on to remain in this world.

Experiences like this convinced me that reconnecting to our creativity is one of the mightiest healers, even if we've hit rock bottom. These courageous people reminded me of creativity's sheer strength and that we can all access it even in the direst of situations. Through these people's eyes, I saw that creativity's most powerful function is not to impress or please others. It is to return you to your true self.

> Creativity's most powerful function is to return you to your true self.

Now in my early twenties and hungry to maintain my newfound yet precarious strength, I began to study the practices of great artists and thinkers, as well as cultural movements of the past. I was astonished as a vast network of intertwining philosophies that have been all but lost lit up my consciousness. These forgotten philosophies — many tapping into the power of nature herself, such as traditional Celtic beliefs and the transformational insights of ancient Egypt — married with inspiring global creative practices, such as the Indian classical music model of apprenticeship, to birth my philosophy, the Bright Way creative path you are about to embark on.

BRIGHT WAY ACTIVITY
Who Supports You?

Just as my many allies have helped me, I hope to be your ally as we traverse this Bright Way together. What other allies have been quietly gathering around you? Take a moment to reflect. Who has been silently supporting you over the years? Even someone who gave you one word of encouragement counts.

When I consider my allies, I realize they all have a common quality: they are purveyors of growth. They believe we can grow and flourish at any time, any place. Limitations, as much as these sage allies acknowledge them, are treated as opportunities for growth, not permanent states or indictments. Who in your life has believed in you and pointed out your constant potential for growth? You may well have a fleet of guardian angels that you never noticed before. Write these names and energies down, for your eyes only.

During the unavoidable challenging moments this school of life throws at us, look at your list of allies and feel heartened. You may even feel inspired to deepen your relationship with them, now that they have emerged from the shadows!

If no one or nothing pops to mind, try this exercise: stand up, close your eyes, and feel your feet firmly planted on the ground. Sense each foot in complete contact with the ground. Spread your toes out confidently into the earth. Notice the implicit trust that you'll stay rooted to the floor rather than fly off. Feel Mother Earth's unconditional support of you, her gentle presence holding you. You don't have to grasp for or earn this support. Simply because you are alive, Mother Earth is here as your constant ally. Gather strength from her love.

Heart Connection Practice

In this spirit of recognizing allies and honoring connection, now is the perfect time to tap into your heart energy as a prime source of strength, intelligence, and wisdom. Though this may sound like a lifelong quest, I promise that it's possible to get in touch with your heart energy right at this moment. Your heart, your ultimate ally, is always with you. We're discovering more and more about how much the heart really knows. This was clearly understood in the past with the "cardio-centric" views of ancient Egypt and Greece, which place the heart as the primary seat of intelligence. Let's reclaim this ancient wisdom!

> Your heart, your ultimate ally, is always with you.

We Are Here in Love

Try this heart-connection practice now. Close your eyes and think of someone, something, or somewhere you love unconditionally. Easy choices are family members, pets, holiday spots, or anything noncontroversial and joyful for you. Fill yourself with the image and energy of this being, this object or place. Breathe deeply. Feel your heart warm. Allow the sensation in your chest to expand like an infinite balloon. Keep breathing. Keep loving. Keep warming.

If you can't think of anything you love unconditionally, try this: put your left hand over your heart and close your eyes. Pause. Connect to your heart's beating. Let a few breaths sink in. Repeat out loud, "We are here. We are here in love. We are love." Feel your heart courageously pulsating, your steadfast friend. Feel its unconditional love as it gifts you life itself.

Now open your eyes and notice how you feel. Do you feel more hopeful, loving, trusting, strong? Whether or not you do, take heart: you're already well on your way simply by initiating this practice. You'll learn how to connect with your heart energy more fully in step one. Practice even now as you read these passages by keeping your heart energy open and engaged. This is *your* path. Trust your heart as your mind and spirit's surest ally.

BRIGHT WAY ACTIVITY

First Love

Do you remember the moment you first fell in love and connected with your art (which could be anything from painting landscapes to baking cakes)? Do you remember getting lost in an activity, that thrill of total engagement? How did you feel about yourself? Did you feel strong, excited, or another intense sensation? Write down your memories from these moments, as emotionally and viscerally as possible.

There are many benefits to writing down your feelings and thoughts, from greater insight to increased follow-through. Keeping a creative diary will be one of our main tools on our journey, and you'll learn more about this artistic ally in the "Bright Way Spiral" chapter. For now, write in whatever is handy, and we'll collate your work in the diary shortly.

❖ ❖ ❖

The Principle of Sacred Reciprocity

Your human creativity enables you to wield massive power, a power that affects almost every element and living thing today. How you use that power is up to you. Sometimes people fear that when they open the creativity floodgates, terrible things will be unleashed, as in the myth of Pandora's box. They cite the creation of the atom bomb as one of the worst examples of this. They see it as the ultimate example of creativity gone wrong, of creativity in service to life destruction rather than life affirmation.

I understand this valid concern. I'm grateful when people bring it up because it ushers in a key principle of the Bright Way. There is a way to ensure you create from a place of positivity, heart-centeredness, and life affirmation rather than life destruction. It's a technique I use every day to guide me toward creating with love, not fear. What is this creativity safety valve? It's called Sacred Reciprocity. The energy of Sacred Reciprocity weaves through every page of this book.

Sacred Reciprocity is a South American wisdom philosophy with parallels in most other cultures and eras. In a nutshell, Sacred Reciprocity is the force that seeks balanced relationship in all things so that healthy life can flourish.

> Sacred Reciprocity is the force that seeks balanced relationship in all things so that healthy life can flourish.

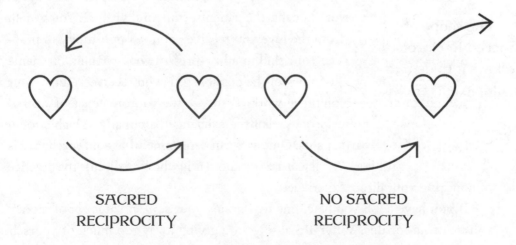

SACRED RECIPROCITY

NO SACRED RECIPROCITY

Figure 1. The Flow of Sacred Reciprocity

Sacred Reciprocity represents an equal exchange of energy that is healthy and helpful for all parties involved. You've probably heard the phrase "everything is interconnected." What does this actually mean? Sacred Reciprocity is an elegant way to grasp and *act on* the aim of honored interconnection in everyday life. The famous Golden Rule, "Do unto others as you would have them do unto you," echoes the tenets of Sacred Reciprocity. The more you look, the more you'll find messages pointing you toward Sacred Reciprocity, hidden in plain sight. Let's look more closely.

We discussed the miraculous power of creativity to reconnect the creator with herself and the world at large. But do all connections lead to life affirmation? What about connections that are toxic? According to Sacred Reciprocity, these are not true connections. Instead they are one-way drains. Sacred Reciprocity is the most reliable tool I know of to assess whether you are in healthy connection.

Sacred Reciprocity is nonjudgmental and clear. It offers this simple yardstick. Ask yourself, *Am I choosing love or fear?* When we are in Sacred Reciprocity we make decisions from a place of love and enthusiasm. And marvelously, an equal balance of love and enthusiasm will return to us in the big picture.

The scope of Sacred Reciprocity, also known as right relationship, allows it to deal in multiple currencies. That is, time and money are not the only ways to get in balance with our creative work — or anything else, for that matter.

> The scope of Sacred Reciprocity allows it to deal in multiple currencies.

For example, if you volunteer at a hospice center, your work benefits the patients, staff, and visitors. You benefit from the love you receive and the opportunity to practice your skill in a low-pressure environment, to name just a few of the possible gifts you receive in turn. Your volunteer work, then, satisfies a core tenet of Sacred Reciprocity, that the exchange be equally valuable to all participants. Only you can determine what equal exchange is for you. We'll learn more about this when we discuss the practice of honoring your direct experience.

If you have a job you hate, one that drains your soul, no amount of money will make up for this. Why? Because you're giving away too much of yourself to be in a healthy balance. Further, you're operating from a place of fear ("What will happen if I give up this soul-crushing job and the steady paycheck that comes with it?"), fear being an additional drain.

There are many permutations of how energy comes into balance. Sacred Reciprocity gives voice to these many dimensions, freeing you up to honor what makes sense for your life both right now and in the long term.

Wisdom traditions of the world have many ways of describing what happens when Sacred Reciprocity is not respected. The original Greek and Hebrew Biblical words for "sin" are *amartano* and *chata*, respectively, which also translate as "missing the mark." In other words, true connection has not been made, and where there is no connection, there is no love. In Hinduism the concept of karma explains how the quality of connection we make leads to either positive or negative outcomes in life. Buddhism takes this perspective: "Every action, good or bad, has an inevitable and automatic effect in a long chain of causes." Pagan spirituality's law of return states that what you put out into the world returns to you threefold — emotionally, physically, and spiritually — recognizing many dimensions, Sacred Reciprocity style.

Finally, you don't have to have a spiritual outlook to live in Sacred Reciprocity: "Humanists believe that this is the only life of which we have certain knowledge and that we owe it to ourselves and others to make it the best life possible for ourselves and all with whom we share this fragile planet." Sacred Reciprocity applies everywhere, a clear guide for our complex times.

BRIGHT WAY ACTIVITY
Sacred Reciprocity

Take a moment to consider how Sacred Reciprocity plays into your life right now. As we walk this path together, you'll learn more about this overarching life philosophy; for now, let's start with a brief environmental assessment.

Think about the three people who are closest to you. Are you in Sacred Reciprocity with one another? If so, your relationships will feel healthy and strong on the whole. (It's good to remember, though, that perfection isn't part of Sacred Reciprocity, as relationships are always changing and rebalancing.) If your relationships don't feel healthy, what currencies might bring these relationships into balance for all parties? Using the Five Love Languages from Gary Chapman's book by the same name can be a fun place to start: Do you need to add more words of affirmation to the relationship? How about quality time, physical touch, acts of service, or gifts?

Sacred Reciprocity honors what is sacred to the relationship as a complete ecosystem; so discern which currencies have value in your particular ecosystem. Honor what has value for you.

Sacred Reciprocity: Collaboration, Not Competition

By its very nature, Sacred Reciprocity fosters a spirit of collaboration rather than competition. We spoke earlier about how connection drives human creativity. This book is an example of collaboration across time and space. When I review all the energies that have come together to make this book possible, it's clear that very little would have happened if a stance of competition had prevailed. So how can we invite more collaboration into our lives?

For many, the workplace is the venue of most competition and strife. If you've been struggling to feel more fulfilled and creative in your job, how can you apply Sacred Reciprocity so that connection is restored? How can you be in greater Sacred Reciprocity with your coworkers, your customers, and your vendors?

Take this stance: create win-win situations. When you negotiate, try to understand what the other side wants and what has meaning for them. Ultimately, what currency has value to them? Acknowledge and try to meet those needs within Sacred Reciprocity, remembering that for balance to be attained, you must benefit, too. So when you draw up a contract, spell out the benefits to both sides. When you write an email, be sure to start with a pleasant acknowledgment so that you're giving as well as taking or requesting.

BRIGHT WAY ACTIVITY
One Small Act of Kindness

It's true that we live in a competitive society, so sometimes it's up to us as individuals to go against the grain and get collaborative energy flowing. Today, try one of these techniques: give a stranger a smile, say thank you with meaning, make eye contact. What other small act of kindness can you perform to show people that we're all in this together?

Go big picture. Look beyond the surface and give something that has genuine meaning for you, no matter how tiny it may seem to the outside world. It could be as small as making someone a cup of tea. Step aside from linear time: Sacred Reciprocity isn't impatiently transactional, and it can be rebalanced at any time. You have much to offer this world besides money and time, both of which can be in short supply on occasion.

Besides showing you what you genuinely value, Sacred Reciprocity also highlights the many valuable energies you possess inside. Examples could be your compassion and enthusiasm, both of which have the power to turn around someone else's day when you share them. Take a moment to turn the kindness toward yourself, and acknowledge the beautiful qualities you possess inside.

Sacred Reciprocity even applies to things we might consider inanimate. For example, how do you approach:

- Your musical instrument / tools of your art? Do you embrace them as respected allies, or do you grab them as objects to do your bidding? Meet your instrument in a spirit of Sacred Reciprocity, and whole new dimensions of artistry, support, and motivation will open up to you.
- Food and cooking? That's always a challenge for me until I acknowledge where all my precious ingredients came from. I think of the

people, places, and elements that came together to make this moment and this dish possible. Magically, when I remember these sources in this way, I'm able to connect from a place of positivity and stop feeling as if cooking is merely a mundane task to be performed.

- Other things in your environment that perhaps you can increase your Sacred Reciprocity with?

Creativity and Sacred Reciprocity: The Fuel-Fulfillment Loop

While the concepts explored here may seem lofty, it's easy to know on a heart level when we are creating in Sacred Reciprocity. When we marry creative engagement with Sacred Reciprocity, we experience the heart-centered sensations of faith and courage. *These can only be felt via direct experience.* This is why active engagement in life is key. No amount of reading can substitute for experience. It would be like trying to describe the taste of an apple to someone who's never eaten one, as my mum once said.

When you're in Sacred Reciprocity, you're functioning from and sharing your highest self. Your true self comes from a source, however you define that mighty energy, whether as God, spirit, higher power, or life force. Your creativity gives form to this great life spirit. Given the magnitude of this, your creative urge must be fulfilled, and your message must be heard, even if by only you.

> Your creative urge must be fulfilled, and your message must be heard, even if by only you.

A void opens in our hearts when we ignore our creative voice. This hole often gets filled with external activities and expectations misaligned with our true selves. We fall prey to the mercy of goods, substances, and other people, immersed in fearful living. We've all been there and will be there again. Yet there are reliable routes out of this dead end. The Bright Way is one of these routes.

Throughout human civilization we have pondered whether the universe is friendly or hostile, or perhaps even indifferent. Living in Sacred Reciprocity, we affirm that the universe is friendly. We know the universe as our beloved collaborator, a perspective that in itself can transform our life for the better. Allow in the positive energy that wants to reach you: lower your shield of fear. Imagine yourself as a solar panel, effortlessly attracting sunny energy. This is available to you right now. We're in this together. My story is your story. Let's make our stories shine bright!

The Bright Way Ignites

Where I am now on the Bright Way path, I feel miles away from when I plunged off that cliff of performance anxiety. Having fallen so low, how did I find the strength to turn this all around, to take action in the first place? Crawling up a cliff after a catastrophic flop feels like a Sisyphean task. Let me say up front: small actions are key, and they often end up having much more significance than we might initially assume. Can you look back on an action that seemed tiny in the moment but turned out to be life-changing for you?

> Small actions are key, and they often end up having much more significance than we might initially assume.

Small Steps

Returning to my story of creative recovery, after the Orbit Room encounter with my mother, my opening for action glimmered. At the very least, I could bring music back into my life for my own enjoyment. Why not give it a try? I rented an upright piano, playing for myself as if for the first time. I relived innocent moments, those times of joy and freedom before the heaviness descended.

My roommates asked me to show them little things on the piano, and I found it fun to share music socially, something that had never occurred to me before. Maybe as a glint of premonition, I had bought a print of Renoir's two girls at the piano even before my return to the instrument. Seeing the Renoir girls in this newly dawning light, absorbed in making music for its own sake, enjoying each other's company as my friends and I did, gave me hope. I posted a teaching flyer, and a few students showed up. Sharing music was my sole agenda. It was tremendous fun, and to my surprise I found I was actually a decent teacher. More students came, and my studio grew.

BRIGHT WAY ACTIVITY
One Tiny Action

One small action can change your life. When my roommates asked me to play them one of the songs from the movie *The Piano*, unbeknownst to any of us at the time, they were pointing me toward a new way of life. By taking a few minutes and playing them a few things, I set wheels in motion that ultimately led to the writing of this book.

Take one tiny action step today in service of your creativity. Call that teacher you've been considering for a preliminary hello, attend an open mic, go to an art opening, agree to share a little part of your wisdom with someone. Pay attention to small signs and openings. Today something magical will happen if you open your heart to it.

While I delighted in witnessing my students' pleasure in playing, I was shocked to discover how common performance anxiety and general self-doubt were. I thought I'd been suffering alone, but my students showed me that I was in good company. Looking at them from the outside, I could see their potential straining to burst out. Yet I also felt the barrier of fear holding them back. They were mirrors to me, reflecting that fear is the most formidable opponent to our creativity.

> Fear is the most formidable opponent to our creativity.

Fear takes many forms: as anxiety, shame, guilt, regret, self-doubt, and overwhelm, and many targets: as criticism, loss, and lack, to name a few. A funny thing about fear, though, is that although it seems strong, it actually has very little power unless we fuel it. I understand how hard it can be to step aside from fear. But as in many epic tales, creative victory is yours when you recognize your true power. Everything you need is already inside you and within reach.

BRIGHT WAY ACTIVITY
Reflect on Your Strengths

Tapping into the idea that what you need is already inside you and within reach, take a moment to reflect on your strengths. This might feel awkward at first; we're often much more comfortable detailing our perceived weaknesses. Start building up your inventory of positive personal qualities. Are you kind? Enthusiastic? A keen focuser? Write down your findings, for your eyes only.

Spurred on by allies near and far, present and past, I took up piano lessons again shortly after graduating from the university. I struck gold with my first phone call, to Amelie. To cut a very long story short, by focusing on the joy-centered Suzuki Method — which I'll describe later — Amelie helped me take my first baby steps toward dissolving my fear of performing. Finding this footing gradually led to the jump of pursuing a master's degree in classical piano performance. A bold move, this leap involved bypassing the entire bachelor's degree program.

> Everything you need is already inside you and within reach.

Immediately after the audition for the master's program, a formidable concert pianist named Roy Bogas stepped away from the jury and approached me directly. I braced myself to hear, "You know, this might be a bit too much for you." Instead, I stood agape as Roy smiled and took my hand: "I can see what you're trying to do, and I like it. I want to be your teacher."

After recovering from this head-spinning turn of events, I couldn't blurt out *yes!* fast enough. I count this among my most blessed moments in life so far, and I'm honored to bring Roy into your life as a Bright Way ally. Roy's philosopher-king approach to music study is full engagement: to him, music is about connecting to human experience and giving it full vent. His skill level is just as impressive as his artistry. Among the many lessons I learned from Roy is that skill and magic must come together in order to create meaningfully.

> Skill and magic must come together in order to create meaningfully.

Honoring only skill or magic — being concerned only with technique or, conversely, focusing solely on expression — leads to incomplete creation. If you've been wondering why your creative work doesn't satisfy you, marrying your skill and your magic is a major piece of your puzzle. While skill is self-explanatory, magic by its nature is more mysterious. Yet you can discover and cultivate your magic deliberately. Our journey will show you the way, along with helping you elevate your skill.

As I got a firmer hold on how to create in the real world rather than just in my hopes and dreams, disasters stopped happening. I could handle low-key performances such as providing background music for cocktail hours. But what about the higher-pressure stuff, such as the master's program recitals that I couldn't avoid? Those still felt terrifying. Slogging along, I experimented with every solution that crossed my path.

You name it, I tried it: therapy, off-label beta-blockers, yoga, Alexander Technique, the Feldenkrais Method, exposure therapy, meditation, research into the history of performance practice worldwide, sports psychology, commiserating with others in the same predicament, tricks such as picturing the audience naked, and spiritual practices of many paths and eras. Staring at the Berkeley Zen Center's blank wall, legs numbing under my hard little cushion, I questioned if all this was actually working, meanwhile trying not to picture anything funny in that roaring silence. And over time, I found that my experiments were paying off, albeit in a two-steps-forward-one-back fashion.

The Bright Pattern

In my early thirties at this point, I noticed a pattern emerging from these experiments. This pattern turned out to be stunningly simple. I shouldn't have been surprised, given that I was drawing from so many wells of wisdom across cultures and throughout time. When I was a child, my parents got rid of the television as soon as they realized we kids were becoming addicted to it. So my siblings and I took charge of our entertainment, and my parents' wondrous library of art and history books and records was a regular port of call. In those stacks (which are still growing!), we were privy to the confluence of art and history: looking at ancient Egyptian art automatically meant learning about that culture's philosophical practices. We learned how Ireland kept the flame alive during the Dark Ages via illuminated manuscripts. We heard Enlightenment attitudes crystallized in Mozart's music. The Great Truths are universal, and the primacy of the creative urge is right up near the top of our human truths, as the outpouring of creativity past and present attests to. It makes complete sense that there would be a known pattern for manifesting human creativity, albeit not always widely known.

The pattern revealed to me was this: *there are simple ways to access and follow through on creativity*. These simple ways are ready to break their hermetic seal so all can know them and live joyously by their truths. These truths are embedded in the Five Bright Way Steps you'll be taking soon. While it may seem startling that reigniting your creativity and following through on it can be boiled down to a mere five steps, I'm here to assure you that many others have achieved this, and you can, too. Let me share a little more about how I came to distill down to this level of simplicity.

Sharing the Bright Way

Tentatively, I started to share my findings with my students. One by one, using these discoveries, they achieved performance breakthroughs to such a degree that I had to discard any belief in innate talent. I've witnessed too many seemingly miraculous revelations of artistry, expression, and inspiration coming out of the blue, even from supposedly hopeless cases. I'm utterly convinced that all people are creative and, further, that we must express this creativity in order to be fulfilled as human beings.

Lessons Learned

I remember one teenage student who always played with a staggering lack of expression, even after two years of dedicated work together. I tried my best, yet I have to admit that some part of me had given up hope. Then suddenly, one day she walked in, sat down, and played gorgeously. I was stunned by her transformation. Remorse hit me for believing there were limits to her abilities. For a brief period I debated internally whether I should continue teaching, given the immensity of my mistake.

Pulling myself together, I swore on the spot to never again judge anyone's level of so-called talent — and I highly recommend that you insist your mentors embrace this same perspective. From then on, I would share the message that growth is *always* possible and that every single person has creativity inside them, waiting to be set free. I've witnessed amazing turnarounds many times since that fateful day. This wasn't a fluke; it was a revelation.

Both personally and from the standpoint of being a teacher, I've experienced the massive impact mentors have on our creative lives. It is important to pause here and reflect on the mentors in your life, because they play a significant part in your creative journey. People in these sacred roles include teachers, coaches, instructors, and guides and represent intimate relationships not to be entered into lightly. You've seen how my mentors affected me. As you move forward on your creative path, allow me to share my recommendations for selecting your mentors so that you both flow in Sacred Reciprocity:

1. Mentors are growth-oriented at every moment; move on immediately if you feel any type of constriction or negativity coming your

way. I don't mean constructive criticism here! Constructive criticism is both positive and necessary in order for us to break out of ruts and habits and to see past blind spots. Accurate, even somewhat bracing, feedback is absolutely fine (and often the trigger for a breakthrough!) if it is delivered with discernment and love.

2. Mentors are highly skilled at what they teach; they demonstrate their ability to do *and* understand their subject.

3. There is chemistry between you and your mentor. Trust your intuition. Mentors have such a grand impact on our creative lives that the entire skill-magic trajectory must be honored. While your mentor must be skilled, there must also be magic between you. Hold your mentorship relationships to the same high standards you would your intimate relationships.

BRIGHT WAY ACTIVITY
Review Your Mentors

Review all your past and present mentors. Do they fit all three recommendations above (they're growth-oriented, they're highly skilled, and there's chemistry between you)? If so, detail how they fit and what effects that had on you.

Conversely, if they didn't fit, what effect did that have on you? Please don't get distressed during this activity: many of us have endured nonideal mentors, myself included. As composer and producer Emma said, "It was an enormously healing step for me to acknowledge the impact of traumatic mentors and that I actually had some creative trauma. It felt really therapeutic for my creative reclaiming to journal it out and not dismiss it."

Review your list, and meditate on this: you have just drafted the job description of how to be your best mentor. Relish the rise in confidence you might feel as you step into this role more and more.

From this place of small yet mighty actions, growth mindset, and Sacred Reciprocity, it's time for you to take the Bright Way Readiness Quiz!

The Bright Way
Readiness Quiz

Our journey together will ask some things of you. It will ask straightforward questions to spark and guide you. More deeply, it will ask you to look inside and *act* on this Great Work. In the state of body-mind-spirit wisdom we've cultivated so far, please ask yourself these questions:

> *Am I ready to lay aside old ways of seeing and doing things in order to try out this new path wholeheartedly, at least temporarily?*
>
> *Am I ready to sit in the unknown and allow the known to come forward in its own time, without rushing it?*
>
> *Am I ready to tolerate some possible confusion, even frustration, as this new way of seeing and doing things takes shape?*

If I am used to relying on my intuition, am I ready to welcome the practical onto my journey?

If I am used to being practical, am I ready to start reconnecting with my intuition?

If I become stuck, am I ready to reach out for help? (Remember your list of allies from the Bright Way Activity on page 18.)

If you answered yes to most or all of these questions, then you stand to get a lot out of our journey together. Learning new things and changing old habits can feel scary and uncomfortable. These feelings are actually auspicious signs showing that you're growing, not simply retreading familiar ground. If you can embrace the above attitudes before we start, the shock of the new won't be as severe and you'll enjoy our trip far more.

If you answered no to any of these questions, I encourage you to come along anyway! Which of the questions can you say yes to? Every journey starts from somewhere. Welcome to this new way of life, and thank you for giving it a try.

Let Hildegard of Bingen be your ally going forward: "Dare to declare who you are. It is not far from the shores of silence to the boundaries of speech. The path is not long, but the way is deep. You must not only walk there, you must be prepared to leap."

The Bright Way
Revelation

Arriving where I am today was a messy, long, exciting, excruciating, and ecstatic process, featuring major pitfalls. That's because I navigated without a dedicated guide, piecing together wisdom from sources both ancient and modern; dear teachers; feedback from beloved students, collaborators, and friends; and assistance from the mystery that is life itself.

And here's the most surprising thing of all: *While I thought my biggest fear was of the unknown, of losing control, of being horrified by the darkness inside and around me, it turns out that darkness had been my friend all along.* Darkness, my most cryptic ally, pointed me toward light and connection. Darkness showed me — and still shows me — the Bright Way.

Darkness Faced

What do I mean by "darkness"? I *thought* my darkness was my unspeakable fear that my life had no meaning. My nightmare that I was worthless unless I performed outstanding, heroic feats to justify my existence. My terror that perhaps I was not equipped to meet those challenges. I remember feeling literally dizzy with horror as those fears rose up to haunt me time and time again, undead and relentless. If you are experiencing any of these dreadful anxieties, I want to assure you right now that there is light at the end of the tunnel. But first we must face our darkness, face our unknown: redemption lies within. I am here with you, walking through these shadows, as we move toward a brighter path.

I finally faced my greatest darkness in a most shocking manner. Once a year the oncology department at Oakland Children's Hospital in California has a memorial for the children under their care who have died that year or any previous year. The parents and staff gather in a large room and share stories and pictures.

This was my second time playing harp for this gathering, and although I'd found it emotionally challenging before, I thought I was strong enough to handle it once more. But this time, looking out at the sea of devastated parents, many of whom I recognized from the year before and looked as grief stricken as ever, combined with watching the heartbreaking slideshow of little children smiling in their hospital beds while hooked up to huge machines — some covered in bandages, many bald — catapulted me straight into the darkness I'd tried to avoid for so long.

A tidal wave of grief poured over me, and although I was able to keep playing, I was crying almost uncontrollably. Life appeared a carnage of lost hope and meaninglessness. It was all I could do to get myself to the car, and shaking all the way home, I spent the next three days in a full-blown crisis. I couldn't eat, drink, or sleep, and I trembled in literal mortal terror. Picturing all those sweet children gone forever, I felt I was teetering on a void of nothingness. I fought and fought the looming darkness, desperately pulling out my books by everyone from Thich Nhat Hanh to Starhawk to Hildegard, finding no comfort and no relief. I felt I was losing my mind.

After three long days, exhausted on every level and at the end of my rope, I surrendered my fight. And there I lay, staring into the darkness of death with no fear. No fear, because I had nothing left to fight with. I entered the darkness and accepted that in all honesty perhaps there really is nothing. We live, we die, that's it.

And right at that moment I felt it! A little flame lit up inside my chest, merrily burning away. I leaped upright in the bed in one bound, laughing and crying and filling up with the bright energy of my little flame. I felt my soul shining within me, as it had always been doing. I *felt* my soul without a shadow of a doubt, and I *knew* it beyond any debates or rationales. In an instant I realized that *all my fears were in fact the very things that had disconnected me from knowing my soul, my true self.* When I finally let go, when I let the darkness — the infinite unknown — in, my greatest connection illuminated immediately. My fears evaporated. I feel this same flame connection today, and it is one of the reasons I know that when we face the unknown, we will be liberated by it.

> My fears had disconnected me from knowing my soul, my true self.

I have learned through hard-won experience that if we can dwell in the unknown, sit with uncertainty, if we can face our pain, then healing and transformation can happen. Light and dark, like yin and yang, do not compete with each other. Rather, they complete each other. In fact, they *amplify* each other as beloved collaborators that exist along a spectrum. The spark of initiation is received by fertile grounds, and blossoming into form, sparks further inspiration in turn.

Fear — the very fear that was blocking me from knowing my true self — is both a symptom and a cause of disconnection. Further, living in fear attracts greater fear. Living in fear constricts our lives as it paces around us, imprisoning us in ever-tighter circles.

Darkness does the opposite: it provides the rich intuitive ground for life to take root in and flourish. Darkness facilitates life affirmation of unfathomable depth. Imagination blooms.

Yet facing darkness is not without its challenges. This is why I created the Bright Way: as a path to guide you through the cycles of light and dark that is this creative life. Cycling between intuition and rationality, action and receptivity, the known and unknown, light and dark, individuality and community, you will become a creative alchemist transmuting lead into gold. You will turn the leaden weight of disconnection into the shining gold of your internal flame.

Let's not fear the darkness. Instead, let's face it together. You are not alone on this path.

Connection is what we crave as humans. True connection — connection based in Sacred Reciprocity — is, in a word, love. And that is what this Bright Way has gifted me: a path to choosing love over fear, connection over disconnection, collaboration over competition. We light our flames together, shining bright against a velvet background of deep mystery and all potential.

> The Bright Way is a path to choosing love over fear.

Shining Light on the Shadows

On all epic journeys, there is a moment of hesitation. Let's face that uncertainty, knowing now that it is an ally we have much to learn from. This darkness is an invitation to go deeper. This darkness is an initiation.

Perhaps something like this is surfacing for you: "Since creativity reflects our true selves back to us, what will I see?" This notion can set nerve-racking expectations that your creations instantly be amazing, given that they reflect your very core. Or maybe we worry that there is no real creativity inside us and we will produce nothing pleasing, even to ourselves. Or we might fear that reflections of our anger, worries, and other "negative" emotions look unflattering, resulting in deprivation of love and connection. Indeed, there are many things we might feel anxious about.

The important thing to remember as you go through this process is that the products of your creativity reflect only part of you. They are not actually you.

> The products of your creativity reflect only part of you. They are not actually you.

I remember back when my whole identity was wrapped up in being a musician. Whatever state my music was in, that's how I felt about myself as a person. If things were going well musically, I felt great. If they were going badly, I felt worthless.

What I didn't realize at the time was that my musical output wasn't me, any more than your reflection in the mirror is actually you. Your work is a snapshot in time. A very important snapshot, true, but not your actual soul. Even your creative journey is not you; rather, your creativity is a way back to your true self.

My Bright Way Vision for You

My vision for you is that your creativity shall be your life ally from now on. My dream is for you to engage wholeheartedly with your life, know personal fulfillment, and shine your light back on our world. My hope is that your dreams guide you again — as they once did back in your golden age, no matter how briefly — and that you live your desires out loud from now on. This path is a way to manifest it. Whatever your chosen form of expression, it is your birthright to be creative and live your truth. You *can* live a connected, engaged life, whatever your current and ever-changing circumstances.

I'm here to assure you: your creativity is alive and wants to emerge in all its glory...for *you*. Yes, others may enjoy, admire, and benefit from your work, but it's by keeping a firm focus on your creative purpose *for yourself* that you'll thrive and stay true to your path. If I had to boil down everything we're focusing on here to one message, it is this: creativity is a way of life, not merely a goal.

> You *can* live a connected, engaged life, whatever your current and ever-changing circumstances.

BRIGHT WAY ACTIVITY
Creativity Is a Lifestyle

Write "Creativity is a way of life, not merely a goal" on several sticky notes and place them in your planner, on your bathroom mirror, in your car, and anywhere else you visit often. Notice how the layers of this message's meaning unfold for you. They're still unfolding for me, even after all these years!

As a consequence of walking this path, your work will become more powerful, and more beautiful, and you will achieve things you've always longed for. Products will happen and goals will be achieved naturally along the way as milestones of accomplishment. Yet in the end, creativity is the reflection of your ever-evolving, connected, true self; a traveling star, not a fixed point.

> Creativity is the reflection of your ever-evolving, connected, true self; a traveling star, not a fixed point.

When you choose to activate your creativity, you affirm all life, not just your own. You take up your torch in the procession of human civilization as a creator, not merely as a consumer. You connect with the flow of all who came before us. You set the stage for those who will follow us.

We are the universe creating itself. Even the smallest act of creativity echoes through the sweep of human existence. The first person to recognize the beauty of a plucked bow string didn't know they were setting the stage for the invention of all stringed instruments. Where would we be without that person today? We need you, even if you don't think you have anything earth-shattering to share. One tiny thing you create tomorrow may be the answer to something crucial a hundred years from now. Or it may not be! It's not your worry, either way. You just have to show up and connect with life. *You are enough*. Rudyard Kipling, author of *The Jungle Book* and constant inquirer into the interplay between structure and freedom, concluded: "No price is too high to pay for the privilege of owning yourself."

When we see someone — like *you* — step into their true power, it's the most thrilling thing. We witness magic coming to life. Our faith in humanity is restored. As we reclaim our inborn courage, our love radiates out far and wide, connecting us to everything around us, making sense of life.

> The magic is already inside you.

Now, this might feel like a lot. Do you wonder where to even start on our epic journey? Take hope: the magic is already inside you. Hildegard of Bingen is again with us: "Humanity, take a good look at yourself. Inside, you've got heaven and earth, and all of creation. You're a world — everything is hidden in you." Let's reveal you!

The Bright Way Philosophy

Past Wisdom + Present Illumination

As your final stage of initiation into the Bright Way, it's time to master the philosophical basis of the Bright Way System. This sets you up with the optimum mindset, that body-mind-spirit knowing, for our journey together. It also provides a lighthouse to reorient by as you navigate the creative life's ups and downs.

The Bright Way System is a confluence of two mighty sources. The first is what I call "past wisdom," that vast archive we have assembled as a civilization. This Bright Knowledge is "a great treasury of learning, knowledge, and wisdom, a candle that was eternally renewed as the light passed from recipient to recipient so that a brighter light might illuminate the world."

The second Bright Way source is what I call "present illumination." This represents intuition, sudden knowing, sensing beyond what is rationally learned and categorized. The Old Irish word *imbas* (pronounced IM-bus) means "vision that illuminates" or "instant illumination." It has parallels in many cultures and eras, such as the intense enlightenment experienced upon emerging from Plato's Cave. In order to access intuition, we first sit in darkness, either literally or metaphorically, inhabiting the unknown. In the shadows, we wait agenda-less for whatever wants to be revealed. In this open, intuitive state, we become receptive to sudden bright flashes of insight. Breakthroughs and quantum leaps of understanding become possible. We let go of everyday consciousness, even past wisdom that we might hold sacrosanct. New ways of thinking, being, and feeling flood in, uncensored. New possibilities open up, new ideas and inspiration appear, seemingly out of nowhere.

> The Bright Way respects the past, integrates the present, and calls on you to engage with the grand design.

Light and dark marry: past wisdom lights our way through knowledge while present illumination provides the fertile darkness our intuition requires to take root in. The Bright Way respects the past, integrates the present, and calls on you to engage with the grand design.

All these dimensions synergize with one another. Combining the skill of historical knowledge — not some moth-eaten museum exhibit, but a living, breathing manifestation of distilled human experience — with the magic of present-day experience, you add to the conversation as much as you listen to it and take it in.

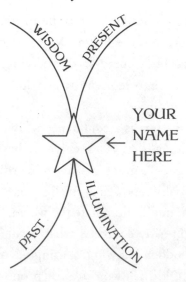

Figure 2. The Intersection of Past Wisdom and Present Illumination

When we look back, it's astonishing how profoundly the sages of the past understood human nature and what it takes to live a meaningful life. Aristotle's and Hildegard's words are as fresh to us as if they lived today, not thousands of years ago. Much of this knowledge went underground and was rarely taught in standard education forums anyway. Now is our opportunity to reclaim this wisdom of the past, grow from it, *and add to it*. History doesn't simply act on us; we create it, every moment of every day. This is our moment.

BRIGHT WAY ACTIVITY
Your Hopes and Dreams

What do you dream of creating? Now that we've come this far together, take a moment to tap into your new hopes and dreams. What do you hope to achieve on our journey together, knowing what you know now? Write down your thoughts. They don't have to be big, and they will not be set in stone. The intention here is simply to enter your Bright Way stream.

Past Wisdom

Tapping into these ancient wisdom traditions, I have grown keenly aware of the real people who laid the paths we walk today. When it comes to classical piano, my longest-existing passion, I connect with the souls of the great composers and to the hopes and dreams of their entire cultures. Playing the exact notes Chopin and Beethoven wrote, I commune with them mysteriously across time. These are real, tangible energies. I learn from them. They directly transmit feelings and beliefs that are still relevant today and worth remembering.

I feel Chopin's vulnerability exposed in every song he wrote. He reminds us that when we share from the heart — even if it's terrifying, as his early retirement from public performing attests to — our work becomes timeless and universal. Beethoven inspires me with his faith in the towering dignity of humanity. His music became increasingly compassionate as he matured, despite the fact that he was repeatedly disappointed by life and his relationships. Beethoven's profound deafness was just the tip of the iceberg. From his abusive father to his famously unrequited loves to his former hero Napoleon trampling his dream of democracy, Beethoven was frequently heartbroken. Yet he wrote some of the most uplifting, passionate, humane, and heroic music of all time.

Early Influences

Growing up in many countries, I learned that time flows in more ways than how I experience it in California now. Here time often feels concrete, forward-moving, and linear. The old is discarded for the new at lightning speed. In contrast, in my earlier years my life experiences were largely naturally intertwined with the past. In Cyprus, for example, my friends and I attended school on a colonial compound without seeing it as old-fashioned, even as we paraded around in our eighties neon garb. We didn't bat an eye as we careened through millennia, passing a medieval Greek Orthodox church one minute, popping into classical goddess-inspired Aphrodite's Café the next, often in hysterics while getting ready for the disco and New Wave music that same evening.

In school we studied both classics and modern English literature, Eliot and Euripides sitting side by side. We moved naturally between vast swathes of time, allowing us access to universal insights. One of the most striking spots to experience this phenomenon physically is Istanbul, where you can stand in Sultanahmet Square, turn 360 degrees, and take in more than three thousand years of human creativity, from the ancient Egyptian obelisk right up to the modern shops hawking knickknacks. I recommend taking a ride on that head-spinning carousel of time if you can. I remember my own experience there as if it were yesterday.

Greek philosophy and mythology were my everyday companions, and in these pages Plato, Aristotle, and others will speak to you down through the ages. Their voices ring out with truth and understanding, as pertinent today as they were more than two thousand years ago. Artist, scientist, software developer Keith Rowland reflects:

"Seeing the threads that have continued from past to present and are still intact helps me discern which are true. 'There ain't much new under the sun.' Philosophy has helped me in my everyday life. I have been very quick to anger and say things I regretted. I tried and tried to stop that habit but couldn't completely. I finally realized the only way was to change my attitude so that the hair trigger wasn't there to begin with. Wisdom is the best tool with which we can change our attitude. It is applied knowledge. We have a whole encyclopedia of examples from which to learn, from others who went through great pain to acquire wisdom and teach us so that we don't have to endure similar pain."

The Power of Language

Language itself is a keeper of wisdom. Words, whether or not we know their roots, shape our consciousness. This is why words hold incantational, subliminal power. Tapping into the original meanings of our everyday words reveals many secrets. The word *create*, for instance, is related to the Roman nature goddess Ceres (Demeter in Greek mythology). Her name originates from the Proto-Indo-European root *ker*, meaning "to grow." So, at its root, creativity is natural; *creativity is growth!* This confirms one of creativity's great secrets, which we've already touched on together: creativity is a process, not a product. Creativity is growth, not just the fruit, delicious though that is. Heed past wisdom: it holds many such secrets hidden in plain sight.

> Creativity is a process, not a product. Creativity is growth.

BRIGHT WAY ACTIVITY
What Has Inspired You?

What stories from the past have inspired you? Think about fairy tales, books from childhood, movies, paintings, images, song lyrics. How have these shaped and informed your real-life experiences? Great works of art touch on truth and reflect life's meaning back to us. This is why I count even humble works as great, if they tap into universal truth.

When I was a child, I loved the Moomintroll book series by Tove Jansson. Looking back on those books, I see that many of the themes that moved me then still inspire me today. I loved the freedom, the playfulness, the philosophical asides, the drawings, everything! Once in a while I read those beloved books again, and I feel refreshed and affirmed.

What is contained in your store of past wisdom?

Past Wisdom and the Alchemy of the Bright Way

As you know, it's not just past artworks, stories, and cultures that influence and inspire us. Ancient philosophies are also trustworthy guides on the Bright Way. Why? As Keith said, they've been distilled through millennia of hard-won human experience to quickly communicate our deepest truths. While you don't have to buy into any of these philosophies wholesale (there are too many of them for that, and no guide should be followed blindly), they are sharp skill-building tools and potent symbols of inspiration.

Alchemy, for example, is a practice going all the way back to ancient Egypt and the legendary Greek-influenced Hermes Trismegistus. Alchemy's history and impact fan out from what we now know as the Middle East to all of Europe, the Americas and Asia.

On the surface alchemy may seem to be about transforming lead into gold, an impression encouraged by those wanting to reserve this wisdom for a select few (hence the phrase *hermetically sealed*, referring to Hermes Trismegistus). Story and metaphor are among the best ways to communicate profound messages. As such, "lead into gold" is mostly an allegory for transformation. It refers to transmuting the heavy, dull, and toxic parts of ourselves into light, strong, bright, beautiful gold. This process reflects the grand journey of self-realization we all take and that we are walking together now. Alchemical symbols surround us, for example, heading part 1's chapters. The circle-and-dot represents the sun (creative energy) and gold; the wheel-cross, cycles and the physical plane; the infinity sign, eternally renewing life force. These imagination-stimulating symbols also appear in many belief systems and eras, some dating all the way back to the Bronze Age.

On our Bright Way journey, we'll work through the Operations of Alchemy. These processes, to put it briefly, initiate us with fiery ego-taming and conclude with a celebration of our integration as a body-mind-spirit. This evolution becomes a way of life as we spiral through this healing, creative process over and over, reclaiming our internal gold. As Plato reflected, "Love is born into every human being; it calls back the halves of our original nature together; it tries to make one out of the two and heal the wound of human nature."

Whether you are spiritual, scientific, agnostic, or not involved in any of these perspectives, the tenets of alchemy can be stalwart supports. You already encountered As Above, So Below, one of the principles of alchemy, which is the observation that the big picture reflects the little picture, and vice versa. The meaning above the surface mirrors the meaning below the surface. Our inner mind reflects our outer life, and the reverse also holds true. Your creative life reflects your whole life, and your whole life reflects your creative life. Understanding this principle alone can give you great control over your life, allowing you to become its director instead of a passive watcher.

BRIGHT WAY ACTIVITY
As Above, So Below

Start noticing the coincidences, synchronicities, and connections in your daily life, reflecting the concept of As Above, So Below. For example, how does your approach to learning reflect your approach to doing? How does your health affect your thinking? How does your mind affect your body? How does a painting or a piece of music affect your mood? These are all examples of how As Above, So Below can play out in your life.

You don't have to be an alchemist to walk the Bright Way. On this journey you are simply borrowing these time-honored tools and concepts to heighten your learning and creative experience.

Likewise, when you harmonize with yourself in step one (much more about this later), you might recognize centering and meditation techniques used in many Asian cultures. You don't have to take up Zen philosophy or start practicing Hinduism to benefit from the process of centering. This tool and others that you'll encounter on our journey have corollaries across many cultures and time. All are chosen to be flexible enough to fit into your belief system, whatever it may be. Some of these tools are so common that we find them used in everyday life. I initially heard about centering through sports psychology and was charmed to unearth its ancient roots later!

As Above, So Below

Along your Bright Way journey, work with and morph all terms and symbols to fit your personal ethos. Your heart-centered truth, the purpose that you'll uncover during step one, will be your ultimate guide. Father of modern physics and dedicated alchemist Isaac Newton said, "Plato is my friend — Aristotle is my friend — but my greatest friend is truth."

Present Illumination

As you know, your direct experience is key to your Bright Way journey. It's now time to go deeper and connect your direct experience, your "instant illumination," to mysticism. Mysticism is a direct connection with source energy, no intermediary required. Mysticism is heart- and spirit-knowing, intelligence that can't be captured by rational terms alone. It is intelligence of such depth that it is indispensable to leading engaged, creative lives.

Each person experiences mystical energy differently. It runs the gamut from religious experiences to a deep respect for life, from the humanist perspective to psychedelic encounters. You cannot understand this energy simply by reading about it, attending a lecture about it, or hearing someone else's story about it. You can only feel this energy by living it. *You must engage directly in life by opening your heart in order to experience what I call present illumination.* The mystery will only be revealed to you through your direct participation in life.

I have experienced mystery in the form of direct insights such as when I found my internal flame and when I realized how interconnected everything really is (first I had to connect with myself before I could connect with everything else, a theme you'll find throughout our journey together). I'll be sharing more experiences with you on our path. I rely on intuition to make daily decisions, ranging from artistic choices to whether or not to send that email. Some things can only be decided by the heart, not the head; this is mysticism. As pioneering seventeenth-century French mathematician Blaise Pascal said, "The heart has its reasons which reason knows nothing of.... We know the truth not only by the reason, but by the heart."

> The mystery will only be revealed to you through your direct participation in life.

Mysticism is close to the ground and happens in everyday life. It's not some flighty, detached state. Quite the opposite, as Sigmund Freud agreed: "When making a decision of minor importance, I have always found it advantageous to consider all the pros and cons. In vital matters, however, such as the choice of a mate or a profession, the decision should come from the unconscious, from somewhere within ourselves. In the important decisions of personal life, we should be governed, I think, by the deep inner needs of our nature."

BRIGHT WAY ACTIVITY
Mysticism in Action

Thinking back on the major decisions in your life, such as getting married or changing careers or taking up your art, was it your heart rather than your head that led you? If so, you were experiencing mysticism in action. Write down some of these memories and how you felt about them. How did you trust your intuition? How much do you rely on your intuition right now?

Strengthened by your Bright Way foundation of past wisdom and present illumination, let's now preview the steps you'll soon be walking.

The Bright Way
Spiral

Navigating the Spiral

This chapter is your Bright Way System navigation plan. If you get lost or confused along the Bright Way steps, simply return to this chapter for re-orientation.

The Bright Way System honors three essential truths:

1. All people are naturally creative.
2. You must express your creativity to feel whole.
3. Learning how to fully express your creativity is possible at any time, place, or age.

Let's look at *how* these truths will be manifested on our journey together.

An Overview of the Bright Way System

The Bright Way System is designed so that whenever you dip into these pages, you'll be rewarded with inspiration *plus* concrete tools to move your creativity forward. Even if you start out by focusing for only ten minutes a day, you'll get results.

It goes without saying that we lead complicated lives in busy times. Very few of us have a dedicated atelier with unlimited time and resources at our disposal. Even if we did, these alone are no guarantee of joyful or consistent creativity. For sustainable creativity, we need a system. Just as nature functions in ecosystems, so our creativity thrives when underpinned by a system.

For a system to be effective long-term, it must be efficient while also honoring your emotions. On the Bright Way, we travel light; everything has been pared down to earn its status as essential. The Bright Way System is based on fundamental principles. Rather than skimming a collection of temporary tactics, you'll learn a framework of timeless *strategies* that work across time, space, disciplines, and life circumstances, undergirded by firm *philosophy*.

Lay aside worries about immediately absorbing everything in this navigation section. Everything mentioned cycles around. You won't miss out if you don't notice something the first (or the seventh!) time.

As shorthand, keep in mind our guiding Bright Way equation for manifesting your creativity. This is the *how* of making your creativity real in our world. Skill (practical action) and magic (inspiration) are synergistic. Both must be present for sustainable creativity.

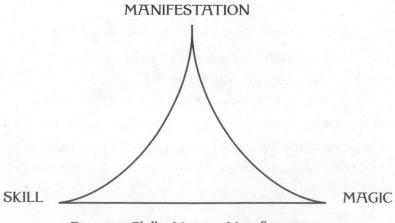

MANIFESTATION

SKILL   MAGIC

Figure 3. Skill + Magic = Manifestation

Now let's meet one of your most important physical tools on our journey: your Bright Way Diary.

Your Bright Way Diary

You might also call this key device your *practice journal*, your *log*, or perhaps even your *grimoire*, seeing as it is your personal skill-and-magic recipe collection. In your Bright Way Diary you'll capture your reflections, questions, and discoveries. You'll log your results and stories. Over time, your particular style and preferred place for writing things down will emerge, much as your learning style will also clarify as we travel together.

What does your Bright Way Diary look like? For now, start with a blank notebook or a pad of paper. Later you can get particular about size, decorations, and features. The choices are as varied as your creativity. Right now, the important thing is to have a place to record your Bright Way findings, for your eyes only.

Digital formats can also work for your Bright Way Diary, but as we'll explore soon, there's a magical power in writing things down by hand. Further, digital formats often change and even become obsolete. See what calls to you right now and what you find easy to rely on. You'll have many opportunities to redraft, as befits the cyclical nature of the Bright Way's learning style. Opt for what works for you today.

BRIGHT WAY ACTIVITY
Diary Time

You have already done some marvelous writing on our path. Transfer your notes into your Bright Way Diary, either by rewriting or by pasting in pages manually. Reviewing your work so far, how do you feel? Lighter? Heavier? Simply note where you are, without judgment.

❖ ❖ ❖

Inspiration Creates Magic; Purpose Kindles the Fire of Inspiration

Though it's easy to understand that skill can be built, the *how* might be a mystery. This is why we focus on specific skill strategies on our Bright Way. But can magic also be deliberately cultivated? Yes! Magic is grown through inspiration.

Let's back up and examine exactly what I mean by magic here. Magic lends spirit to your creativity, infusing it with soulfulness and higher meaning. Magic elevates the matter at hand beyond being merely impressive, pretty, diversionary, or unusual. Instead, it reflects what life means, whether that be in a homespun corner of the everyday such as an intimate folk song or via the most towering pillars in our society, as in Plato's *The Republic*. This magic goes beyond the intellectual and often can't be put into words alone (another reason that art is so important to us!). While magic lives beyond the rational, you can work with inspiration actively — consciously — to bring your magic to life.

Don't worry if any of this sounds enormous, vague, or esoteric to you. There are many tangible ways to cultivate your inspiration, specific techniques for accessing mighty and mysterious energies safely in real life. These techniques, such as accessing your heart energy, which we practiced earlier, have been known throughout the ages and are time-tested and trustworthy. We'll be examining and refining these techniques throughout our journey together.

The primary source of your inspiration is your purpose, that mystical marriage of body, mind, and spirit. Your purpose is what ultimately fuels you and guides your way. Your purpose kindles the fire of your inspiration, the first material of your creativity. This is what you'll experience on our journey together.

Action Creates Skill

Without action, we can't build the necessary skill to express what we feel inside. We can read about something, we can even know something intellectually, but until we take action on it, we won't grow skilled at it. Without skill, your creative feelings stay locked inside you, and communication stops. Skill frees your creativity into the real world. While inspiration/magic is our intuitive side, our action/skill side represents forward movement and practicality, what is traditionally thought of as yang energy and structure.

Discerning what action to take to build your skill can be confusing. Do an online search for guidance, and you'll be bombarded by a thousand tips. What concrete actions actually improve creative skill?

By acting on our Five Bright Way Steps in order and infusing them with the Five Essential Elements of daily practice (we'll be delving into these shortly), you *will* build skill. And this isn't a one-size-fits-all solution. You'll actively craft your own version of this system as you walk this path, honoring your purpose and creative learning styles.

BRIGHT WAY ACTIVITY
Your Guiding Equation

In your Bright Way Diary, draw the skill-magic-manifestation diagram pictured on page 56. Trace the lines with your finger. Say the names of the poles out loud. Feel the flow of energy between the poles. Don't worry about understanding everything intellectually right now. Simply enjoy getting in touch, literally, with your guiding equation! Your magic is growing.

Skill + Magic = Ongoing Creativity

We need both skill and magic to create sustainably, but I've noticed that creatives tend to divide themselves into either skill or magic camps. I hear, "Oh, I'm very practical; I'm not imaginative" or "I'm a feelings person; I don't like to get locked into structure." Our culture encourages these attitudes by dividing people into either "artistic" or "practical" types. But this diminishes us.

For example, free-spirited creatives who prioritize inspiration are adept at flowing with intuition. They live magically, touching on that meaningful something we all know when we feel or see it. It's the life-affirming spirit that moves all of us at the deepest level, whether we're a spiritually inclined person or a dedicated humanist. These magical creatives tap into their illumination with ease. However, they're sometimes frustrated by a lack of practical ability that holds them back from shining their light in full. They get discouraged easily. They push too hard in futile directions, burning themselves out by throwing energy behind fads promising quick results that rarely pan out. Most distressing of all, without the support of skill, their great propensity for inspiration usually dims over time.

When magical creatives increase their skill level, the synergy is electric! As singer-songwriter Kate Magdalena Willens makes this discovery, her excitement is palpable: "I have deprived my musical life of inspiration at times that I have viewed structure as something dry and uninteresting, and only inspiration as something juicy and delicious. The truth is that inspiration can be nurtured, strengthened, and developed through structure!"

BRIGHT WAY ACTIVITY
Creating Structure

Do Kate's words resonate with you? If so, can you imagine two ways that having more structure might stoke your inspiration? For example, would setting aside a specific amount of time a day for your creativity help your inspiration flow? Would learning a little about musical theory every day help your inspiration blossom? Write your ideas in your Bright Way Diary.

If you already have structure, can you detail two ways that it creates a helpful container for your inspiration? For example, does your knowledge of baking principles give you leeway to experiment more? Does your understanding of history give you insight into forging a new way forward? Jot your observations into your Bright Way Diary.

On the other hand, many superbly skilled people crave more soul in their work. They possess the technical chops, but something is missing. They don't feel moved by what they create, and others don't seem to react to their efforts, either. These creatives feel left out of the gifted category. Perhaps they believe they just weren't "born that way." Maybe they blame or envy others, without realizing they already hold the answer inside. Inserting soul consciously into your work may seem like an oxymoron — doesn't soul just show up automatically? Unfortunately not: if you wait around for inspiration to strike, you could be waiting a very long time.

The good news is that it's completely possible to cultivate your magic deliberately. If you see yourself primarily as practical, lay aside fears that engaging your intuitive side will unleash chaos. Rather, your work will spring to life! Retired nursing professor Carol says: "I'm practical, and for me that seems to be a dominant mode. It works well for me. But I'm a good explorer and not afraid to try something different as long as I don't think it will hurt me. I think the most helpful thing to me has been that I now feel more freedom to explore. Also, it is very liberating to be exposed to people who aren't rigid about how things should be done. It's refreshing to have some balance."

Scientist, computer engineer, and harpist Amelia says: "I am naturally more right-brained but grew up expecting to be a scientist. I think this has been useful for me in becoming a musician later in life. Nothing works like magic and intuition for igniting inspiration, and at the same time, discipline and structure are very important to keep me focused on my goals."

However you identified in the past, whether practical or intuitive, you don't have to relinquish your admirable qualities. Instead, you'll expand on them by integrating the opposite side of your creative being.

BRIGHT WAY ACTIVITY
Your Creative Type

Which type of creative do you identify as? Are you more on the skilled/rational side or the magical/intuitive side? Perhaps you cycle between these two states already? Take a moment to jot down some of your associations with the two sides of the creativity coin in your Bright Way Diary. Here are some guidelines to assist you:

- What do skill and rationality mean to you? Think of someone or something you consider very practical or analytical. What positive aspects do you associate with them? For example, you might feel that being practical leads to being more organized. Do you attach any negative characteristics to practicality/rationality? For example, you might perceive being practical as being boring.

- Perform this same inquiry for magic and intuition. What positive aspects do you associate with intuition? Perhaps it feels exciting and expansive? Do you attach any negative characteristics to magic and intuition? Do they seem flaky?

This activity is intended to get your skill-magic spectrum feelings out in the open; so be honest with yourself, even if what you feel doesn't "look good." Don't worry about coming up with any paradigm-shifting realizations or actions right now. Simply start examining where you may have allowed limitations into your life. In doing so, you're already starting to free yourself from them.

Skill + Magic = Motivation

Motivation — or lack of it — comes up often in conversations about creativity. More good news: when you marry skill and magic, motivation follows automatically. You no longer have to hunt down motivation or force it. Instead, you'll be sustainably fed by the cycle of inspiration and action. This cycle both accelerates and deepens your creativity. Vast reservoirs of energy open to you when you let go of *force* and embrace *flow* instead. You'll learn exactly how to do this on the Bright Way.

The Confluence of Many Sources

The Bright Way distills a lifetime of learning, performance, teaching, and research into practical and philosophical principles that apply to every art form, to every creative endeavor, and, further, to an artful *life*. Great philosophies of the past and of worldwide cultures infuse our journey, from classical Greek thought to folkloric tales to direct, modern-life experience.

The Bright Way System is ultimately inspired by and connected to the circular flow of nature, our supreme template for creativity and abundance in this world. Let's preview our system before going into depth in later chapters.

The system spins in two interwoven cycles:

Figure 4. Overview of the Bright Way System

The Outer Cycle: The Five Steps

The Five Steps are:

1. Define your purpose
2. Set your intentions
3. Create your practicum plan
4. Integration
5. Fulfillment: the wheel turns again

The Five Steps are a sequential yet circular process; that is, each step builds on the previous one. Moving step-by-step, you gain both momentum and results organically, bypassing the draining actions of personal exertion and external force.

Figure 5. The Five Bright Way Steps

We start with the most important step: define your purpose (step one). Every other step is based on your purpose, so you'll want to take all the time you need identifying that purpose.

Set your intentions (step two) grows directly from your purpose. This approach might be a new way of setting goals for you. It prioritizes your deepest beliefs and values rather than taking cues from external expectations. This makes it easier to direct your daily actions toward your intentions, since you are always in touch with the *why* behind your choices. In our world of endless choices, the ability to focus clearly is a big relief.

You have seen what happens when you hold a glass out to the sun
and concentrate all the rays onto one spot, Zorba?
That spot soon catches fire, doesn't it? Why? Because the sun's power
has not been dispersed but concentrated on that one spot.
It is the same with men's minds. You do miracles,
if you concentrate your mind on one thing and only one.

— NIKOS KAZANTZAKIS, *Zorba the Greek*

Create your practicum plan (step three) is based on your intentions. This might seem surprising; many people set up a practice schedule and then decide what their goals or intentions are. When you start with purpose-driven intentions, drawing up a practicum plan becomes an exciting manifestation exercise rather than a chore.

Integration (step four) entails trying everything on for size. It's about seeing what's working and capitalizing on that, noticing what isn't and remedying that — all from a place of curious observation rather than harsh judgment.

After all this marvelous work comes step five, fulfillment, where you celebrate all your well-earned successes. This is a crucial yet most overlooked step, and you'll learn why when you reach it. Much to look forward to!

As you can see, any amount of time spent on defining your purpose is time very well spent because your purpose is the foundation of your entire journey. For that matter, take all the time you need on any of the Five Steps as you work through them sequentially.

On the Bright Way, there's no rush. There are no arbitrary deadlines (you are welcome to set deadlines for yourself; they can be steadfast allies if employed in service of your creativity rather than as threats). And there's definitely no finish line, since our journey spirals. Think of a Möbius strip or even the circle of life — that's us!

Once you've completed the Five Steps, you spiral around to revisit your purpose, this time with a higher consciousness. From here, you get to set intentions that are even more focused and meaningful to you. Inspiration blooms, and motivation follows naturally. Fulfillment expands.

BRIGHT WAY ACTIVITY
The Outer Cycle

Draw the Bright Way System outer circle diagram in your Bright Way Diary. By doing this, you're already walking the steps!

The Inner Cycle: The Five Essential Elements (and Their Corresponding Natural Elements)

The Five Essential Elements are:

1. Inspiration (Fire) △
2. Artistry (Water) ▽
3. Learning (Air) △̶
4. Technique (Earth) ▽̶
5. Community (Spirit) O

While the steps of the Bright Way System are sequential, the essential elements flow together simultaneously, in coexistence. They bubble as a cauldron of creative energy, each element infusing the other with flavor and spice.

You'll be hearing more about the elements in the following chapters, so don't worry if any of this sounds unfamiliar or feels like too much to remember in one sitting. Let everything unfold at an organic pace, whatever that is for you right now. Honor your personal learning style. With that said, let's preview what the inner cycle is all about.

Figure 6. The Five Bright Way Essential Elements

Just as the five natural elements of fire, water, air, earth, and spirit are the essential, intertwining building blocks of life, *our Bright Way Essential Elements are the lifeblood of your daily creativity*. If one essential element is missing, it can cause breakdowns in learning and creativity. When you reintegrate missing elements, your whole creative ecosystem jolts back to life again.

For example, your writing may feel stuck even though you have a lot of support in the form of community, artistry, learning, and inspiration. However, if your technique is lacking, you might feel like you're trying to write with a broken pen, metaphorically speaking. Technique unlocks your ability to physically manifest what you feel inside. The same holds for each essential element, in that all are vital to making your creation sustainable.

No matter what your creative endeavor, the Five Essential Elements telescope back to the foundations of skill and magic. While each creative field will have its own particulars, all require inspiration, artistry, learning, technique, and community. Pulling back to examine these large spheres of influence gives you confidence that your bases are covered.

The Five Essential Elements are also flexible enough to move with you as your focus changes and your creativity develops. For example, working on choreographing a dance is very different from preparing to perform it. All the while, the essential elements remain by your side, guiding you through every layer of your creative ecosystem.

BRIGHT WAY ACTIVITY
Making Connections

Look at the inner cycle diagram and imagine it as a simmering cauldron of creative nourishment. Trace your finger back and forth between the different flavors, intuitively experiencing the connections between the essential elements. For example, sense how artistry and technique add spice and depth to each other. Allow this activity to be as intuitive or as practical as you're experiencing it right now. Whatever is unfolding for you is splendid.

❖ ❖ ❖

Although the essential elements are constant, they don't have to be in exact proportion to each other. Trying to give each exactly 20 percent of your time would get maddening fast! Instead, check that each is being regularly represented over the space of, say, a week. You'll get the opportunity to practice this and to determine what works best for your creative style as we walk our journey together. For some, using the essential elements every day is key to ongoing engagement. For others, a monthly check-in works better. You'll find your rhythm.

Besides providing the lifeblood to your practice, the essential elements act as *filters*. That is, they help you synthesize large amounts of information into patterns you can act on. Filtering through the essential elements, you can clearly discern what to work on and how to follow through on it all. As you filter your intentions through the elements, you come up with specific actions you can take to manifest them. For example, you'll come up with artistic actions, technique actions, and so on, rather than sitting down and feeling overwhelmed about where to start.

BRIGHT WAY ACTIVITY
The Inner Cycle

In your Bright Way Diary, complete your Bright Way System diagram by drawing in the inner circle. You're already activating your essential elements!

While the essential elements are filters, they are also *amplifiers*. Have you ever felt stuck, not knowing what to do next on your creative path? Perhaps you've sat down to write, only to go blank? Maybe you've put time aside but frustratingly find yourself unmotivated to tend your beloved garden? The essential elements give you a slew of ideas to act on immediately as you consider your art from the five angles of inspiration, artistry, learning, technique, and community. In fact, you might well end up with too many ideas, a kaleidoscope of actions! A delightful problem to have, which will be addressed during step three, where we'll organize your ideas into very manageable practicum plans. Let your inspiration roll now!

Each of the Five Essential Elements has a corresponding natural element to further clarify your focus and spark your imagination (see the Essential Elements Correspondences section on pages 70–74). Reconnecting to the roots of nature reconnects your creative journey to the fundamentals of life. Further, incorporating the natural elements of fire, water, air, earth, and spirit also brings in metaphoric, poetic, universal, and on a very practical level, mnemonic dimensions, deepening your experience on both cerebral and intuitive levels.

BRIGHT WAY ACTIVITY
Drawing the Essential Elements

In your Bright Way Diary, color in the essential element pie pieces, using whatever colors you feel match the natural element correspondences. For example, you might color the inspiration/fire pie piece red (or not — do what moves you). Draw the relevant alchemical symbol ($\triangle$ $\triangledown$ $\stackrel{\triangle}{}$ $\stackrel{\triangledown}{}$ O) on each pie piece (see pages 70–74 for more information).

Take heart: you'll find you've been cross-training for this moment all your life, picking up on the great patterns of creativity behind all existence without even realizing it. Janet Hince, retired licensed professional counselor and now harpist, choral singer, and crafter of all things textile, shares how her garden taught her about creativity:

> "I had a huge vegetable garden for many years. I looked at the inter-relatedness of the physical elements from a growing plants perspective: you must have earth in which the seed can sprout and take root. Water carries everything the plant needs to grow up the roots and stems. You must have air in the earth, both to create space for the roots and to support a community of microorganisms, insects, worms, and mammals that

break down organic matter and release nutrients for the plant to feed on. So there's an invisible community in a garden. Plants must have sunlight, a.k.a. fire, to fuel the process of photosynthesis and convert separate elements into plant material.

"All the physical elements interconnect and all are needed to make a plant grow. Take away any of them, and no plant. Yet beyond or beneath all this is the calling of Life itself, the miraculous and mysterious urging toward manifestation and existence. It calls the first root from the bean seed into the dark, damp earth, that tells some cells to turn into leaves and other cells to turn into stems, and yet others to become a vivid red bloom that after being visited by the community of bees and other pollinators, will transform itself into a scarlet runner bean."

△ ▽ ◬ ▽ O

ESSENTIAL ELEMENTS CORRESPONDENCES

During each step in part 2 we'll focus on one essential element intently. To give you a flavor of each element, I offer these brief examples:

Inspiration = Fire △

Inspiration is the creative spark. It is the initiator and the originator of our creative acts. Similarly, the element of fire embodies passion, drive, and the very dawning of civilization. Fire is powerful, yet it also needs to be tended, both for its own survival and so that it can assist us rather than burn us down. Fire lights our way, warming us with hope and energy. It scorches away the unnecessary.

Here are some examples of inspiration to light your fire of creativity:

- listening to music / going to a concert
- walking in nature / moving via dancing
- reading

- looking at beautiful things
- taking a break

On your Bright Way diagram, trace the alchemical symbol for fire (△) with your finger. Notice how it points upward, just as flames leap up. Feel its energy and notice what sensations, memories, and desires it ignites in you.

Artistry = Water ▽

Artistry takes many forms. Water reflects artistry by flowing through many states, from steam to ice to oceans to clouds. Artistry encompasses the myriad ways we express ourselves. Just as our emotions morph from states of calm to storm, ecstasy to agony, water also shape-shifts. We evolved from water and are largely made up of water. Water is home to our deepest intuition and consciousness. Water is unstoppable, and in many ways, so are our emotions and desires. Water reflects the very polarity of life and death, as does true artistry.

Artistry includes anything that helps you express your vision with emotion. This means knowing what you really want to say and how you want to say it.

Examples of artistry to help your creativity flow are:

- developing your own style by noticing what you love and following that
- cultivating beginner's mind
- developing practices of deep listening and presence
- encouraging flow by tapping into what you love and giving yourself just the right amount of challenge

Again, we'll be exploring specific ways to cultivate all these ideas; this section is just a brief preview.

On your Bright Way diagram, trace the alchemical symbol for water (▽) with your finger. Notice how it points downward, just as water flows down in rivers, waterfalls, and sheets of rain. Feel its energy and notice what sensations, memories, and desires flow through you.

Learning = Air △

Learning means clearly perceiving new material and integrating it into your practice so that it can be recalled and developed. The corresponding element of air supports learning by blowing away cobwebs and bringing a breath of fresh air in the form of new energy, insight, and space. There's nothing like learning to clear and expand your mind, is there? Air clears, from the tiniest detail to the mightiest blocks, so that we are refreshed and available for growth.

Examples of learning for clarifying your creativity are:

- researching how the brain actually learns and then applying those principles
- identifying your unique learning style and capitalizing on it
- adopting a growth mindset in which you believe progress is always possible
- letting go of old habits, experiences, and beliefs that hold you back

On your Bright Way diagram, trace the alchemical symbol for air (△) with your finger. Notice how it points upward yet has a line crossing it. This symbolizes air's urge to rise and also the fact that air is contained within the atmosphere. Feel its energy and notice what freedoms you want to let fly inside you.

Technique = Earth ▽

Technique transmutes all previous elements into reality. By technique, I mean the physical act of doing something as well as the craft and skill sides of creativity. Think of how technique applies to gymnastics or to the craft of pottery or writing a novel. Technique is all about giving things physical shape and structure. Likewise, earth embodies technique by literally grounding and allowing inspiration, artistry, and learning to manifest on the material plane. Earth is our refuge, our rock, the fundamental touchstone we build on. Further, earth expresses itself in ecosystems, mirroring how technique functions in practical, sustainable layers that form an ever-renewing cycle.

Examples of technique for giving your creativity physical form are:

- understanding the nuts-and-bolts skill requirements for furthering your creativity (i.e., mastering gardening practices, learning new communication skills, implementing narrative arc in writing and music)
- retaining an expert instructor in your field for feedback and information
- taking care of your body so that you can manifest your skills with grace
- gathering the best tools of your trade that you can find

On your Bright Way diagram, trace the alchemical symbol for earth ($\triangledown$) with your finger. Notice how it points downward yet has a line crossing it. This symbolizes earth's tendency to descend but also the fact that the molten core of the planet pushes it back up. Feel its energy, and notice how the fire of your desires helps keep you from getting stuck in the mud.

Community = Spirit O

Community is an often unsung yet crucial element of creativity. In my work with creatives over the years, the most surprising revelation to me is how crucial community is. We are social creatures, and without community, our creativity dwindles. Ultimately, community and spirit allow us to encounter Sacred Reciprocity most clearly and to practice and live this philosophy out loud.

What does community actually look like? Your community could be big, small, in person, online, focused on your art, or connected to a completely different part of your life. It could be your family, your chosen family, your local coffee shop, your town, your culture, your heritage, your understanding of how you interconnect as a living being on a living planet. The list is endless, but the feeling of community is clear, even though you can't see it.

Similarly, spirit isn't visible, yet it is often our strongest drive of all when we step back and review our creative arc. Spirit enlivens and supports all the other elements, while having a power of its own. Cultivating our community and our spirit ultimately infuses our creative journey with the mystery of life force itself, from that initial urge, to manifestation, and back again. *This is the soul of your creativity!*

Examples of community for lending spirit to your creativity are:

- forming a writing group / knitting circle / band
- finding an accountability partner
- working with animals and other living beings, such as plants
- listening to someone deeply
- communing with nature

On your Bright Way diagram, trace the alchemical symbol for spirit (O) with your finger. Notice that there is no beginning and no end, symbolizing that creativity is a journey, not a destination. Feel this sense of wholeness when all elements are brought together and infused with spirit.

$$\triangle \; \triangledown \; \triangle\!\!\!- \; \triangledown\!\!\!- \; O$$

How Cycles Naturally Power Creativity

Nature provides us with the model for abundant creativity. Rather than accepting the mechanical pace common in our culture since the Industrial Revolution, we return to nature and emulate her wisdom.

In the natural world, night turns to day, and the year wheels through the seasons. Creativity likewise thrives in cyclical patterns. By connecting your creativity to cycles, you access new levels of energy. This contrasts with the exhausting plod from goal to goal, in which we lose sight of both the big picture *and* the connecting energy between our actions.

You've already encountered Bright Way Activities as allies on our journey, gently prompting you into action and greater connection with yourself. You'll soon encounter Bright Way Breaks. These invite you to pause and recharge. Activities and breaks model the action-receptivity cycle, giving you the chance to practice this dynamic.

Here I'd like to note that Bright Way Breaks are not passive, just as receptivity isn't lifelessly passive. Breaks involve active engagement because you choose and participate in them. A lot happens when you recharge your battery. If you get stuck, frustrated, or tired — all signs you're growing by sloughing off old ways of being — taking a break can jolt you out of a rut and keep your tank topped off. Overwhelm is often fear in disguise. Reroute fear by changing states. Taking deliberate breaks is a reliable way to steward your sanity, so let's practice this now.

BRIGHT WAY BREAK
Gaze at the Earth's Beauty

For our first break, please read these words from our Hildegard of Bingen. (Caveat: never look directly at the sun. Hildegard is writing poetically, not literally!) Spend several minutes with your eyes closed as the messages from Hildegard's words unfold for your life: "Glance at the sun. See the moon and the stars. Gaze at the beauty of the earth's greening. Now, think. What delight God gives to humankind with all these things. All nature is at the disposal of humankind. We are to work with it. For without it we cannot survive.... With nature's help, humankind can set into creation all that is necessary and life sustaining."

BRIGHT WAY ACTIVITY
Project or Journey?

Consider this question: Do you see your creativity as a series of projects or as an ongoing journey? What are the pros and cons of both perspectives? Record your reflections in your Bright Way Diary.

Nature's Secrets for Managing Energy

Nature does nothing uselessly....
In all things of nature there is something of the marvelous.

— ARISTOTLE

I believe that *managing and directing energy* is at the heart of being creative. On my journey to recovery from performance anxiety, I discovered, admittedly with a bit of a jolt, that performance anxiety is the *very same energy that is essential to creating magnetic, impactful performances and works.* The difference lies in how we handle this energy. From this perspective, "conquering performance anxiety" makes little sense. It also explains why attempts to squash stage fright don't work in the long run. This energy is your ally, not your enemy. You don't have to waste another minute battling it. Instead, learn how to use it to grand effect.

> Love is vastly more powerful than fear. Direct your energy toward love; take courage! You'll access nothing less than the power of the universe.

This approach goes for most fear-based feelings. Rather than storming into battle against our fears, thereby endowing them with even more energy, let's use redirection as creative aikido practitioners, to sidestep, outwit, disarm, and reframe fear. By not fueling fear, we get to see it for what it really is. And we have nothing to worry about, because love is vastly more powerful than fear. Where fear closes the door to skill and magic, love throws it wide open. Direct your energy toward love; take courage! You'll access nothing less than the power of the universe.

You Are a Creative Alchemist: Give Form to Your Magic

On the Bright Way, it is an article of faith that you hold massive power within yourself. It's time to unveil *your* magic. Each of us is different. This is a mysterious and marvelous thing. Each of us sees the world from a different perspective. We each have a fresh story to tell. By weaving our stories together, we allow the Bright Knowledge to shine ever brighter, championing life's truth and beauty. Nature again gives us a template for this: picture a fractal spiraling out. We can flow together in a gorgeous fractal, each a distinct yet connected part of the whole. Likewise, the creative path is also a fractal, not a straight line. Keep this image in mind as you traverse our spiral together (and take a peek ahead to page 190 for a literal image to inspire you!).

> The creative path is a fractal, not a straight line.

I'm honored to be your guide, yet I can only point you back toward your real self. It is up to you to take the action necessary to know that self. Yes, receiving knowledge and advice are crucial on the Bright Way, and you will act on these gifts often. Yet creativity must be lived out loud and in the first person.

Your personal experience will unleash visceral insights that no one and nothing else can give you. You can only know your magic through your direct experience. Further, you must recognize and name this magic. This path shows you how.

My charge to you going forward is: honor *your* reality. Trust yourself! Know thyself, Bright One.

BRIGHT WAY ACTIVITY
Invoke Light

You are about to embark on step one. Mark this important moment by invoking light. Light a candle, feel the warmth of a sunrise, glance at sunlight falling on a surface, switch on a light, draw a flame, or perform any other activity that brings light into your life. It's your time to shine.

PART TWO

Step into the Bright Way

Step One: Define Your Purpose

Light Your Eternal Flame

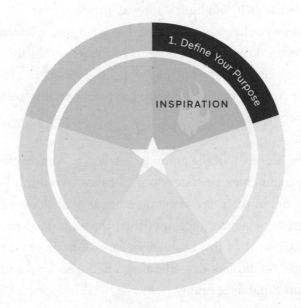

1. Define Your Purpose

INSPIRATION

Y ou've arrived at step one: define your purpose. Your purpose is the foundation of the Bright Way. I can't overstate how important it is for you to connect to your purpose. If there's one thing I want to share with you above all, it is this: connecting to your purpose will change your creative life forever.

Not knowing my purpose made me feel lost and scared. I didn't know *why* I was creating, and more immediately distressing, why I was onstage. Even seasoned creatives struggle with anxiety and confidence when they aren't in touch with their purpose. I would go as far as to say that most people do not know what their purpose is (or that a purpose exists/matters). I believe this is the main reason we see so much performance anxiety and problems with creative flow in our culture.

Rest assured, your purpose resides inside you now, your eternal flame. Your purpose is the fuel *and* the fire that transmute your creative inspiration into tangible action and from there into results. This step will show you how to reclaim your bright purpose.

Fire is your elemental ally during step one. Fire symbolizes burning away the extraneous, including distractions. Your focus sharpens during this step, culminating in defining your purpose clearly. We call on fire to fill you with initiative, comfort you with warmth, and light your way forward.

On our journey *you* become the steward of your potent internal fire. Ayurvedic medicine identifies digestive fire, *agni*, as the key to health, understanding that keeping your internal fire burning steadily is essential for general well-being, as it is for creative well-being. Fire has been our ally from our origins, as writer Jim Gasperini observes:

"We humans, alone of all the animals, learned to control fire.... Wielding fire, we could chase predators out of caves. We think of 'cavemen' as primitive, but in their day wresting control of such useful shelters as caves was an achievement, accomplished through mastery of our first technology. Control of fire enabled us to lose most of our body hair, shrink our gut, spend less time chewing uncooked food and more time exercising our expanding brains.... While we domesticated fire it meanwhile domesticated us. Early on, we learned that to keep the fire going requires cooperative behavior: someone must tend it while others collect fuel. We have probably performed fire rituals longer than we have used language.... To this day, something about lighting a fire, even if just a candle, signifies: now we choose actions with serious intent."

So it's appropriate that our corresponding alchemical operation is *calcination*. During calcination a substance is purified within a fiery crucible, the crucible here being your creative self. Likewise, throughout our journey you'll let go of old ways, habits, and beliefs in order to know and *live* the true you. You'll burn away anything you don't need and reveal the truth of your purpose. Welcome to step one!

BRIGHT WAY ACTIVITY
Invoke Fire △

Turn to the diagram at the start of this chapter. Color in the step one / inspiration pie piece, using whatever color invokes fire for you. Feel yourself get fired up with energy as you do this meditation. If you have no color writing utensils, move on to part two of this activity: draw the alchemical symbol for fire (△) inside the pie piece, even radiating out and up the page. Feel the initiatory energy of the upward triangle, reflecting the striving, heightening nature of fire. Enjoy making your mark on this book, literally! This is *your* journey — make this book yours as well.

How Purpose Illuminates Your Life

Your true purpose is intensely personal. It's possible you will choose to reveal your purpose full force to yourself alone. Expressions of purpose are often one to three sentences long, yet I've also seen them be as pithy as a word, a sound, a symbol, a distinct yet nameless sensation. You'll find yours, as you will discover during step one. Just as only the strongest materials survive the fires of calcination, so will your purpose emerge as a radiant diamond.

Rather than a plain statement of fact, your purpose is heart-based, with universal or spiritual overtones. In fact, your true purpose will often end up being a statement that lights up your entire life, strengthening your will and resilience, and giving you the courage to lower your shields against the world.

Since your true purpose is internal, rest assured that it already glows inside you. No need to search outside yourself for it. Start opening your heart to it.

We have all a better guide in ourselves,
if we would attend to it, than any other person can be.

— JANE AUSTEN, *Mansfield Park*

Purpose wields massive power. Furthermore, purpose is elevated *and* earthy. Knowing my purpose assists me through practical struggles big and small. Like that diamond formed by fire and focus, purpose cuts through to the truth. When I'm swamped with deadlines and demands, or I'm stuck in the weeds, remembering my purpose overrides drudgery. I regain my bearings. We all have hard days, even hard weeks and months. Your purpose is your North Star, shining brightly and reliably, guiding you back when you drift off (which we all do). Do you remember when I said, "Creativity is the reflection of your ever-evolving, connected, true self; a traveling star, not a fixed point"? Your purpose is your fixed point, around which your creativity wheels and turns. Harmony of the spheres!

Your purpose is your North Star, shining brightly and reliably, guiding you back when you drift off (which we all do).

Perhaps you feel skeptical reading this section. *Can purpose really reach this deep?* you wonder. The answer is yes! Your purpose illuminates every aspect of your life, whether you are driving your car or working on your art. I know of a calligrapher whose purpose is "to express sheer beauty," and she does this through everything in her life, from her communications to her cooking to her traveling.

Your purpose may be hearth centered, such as building a beautiful home, tending to your family, or cooking with love. It may be outward facing, such as creating new organizations or works to help your community or humanity in general. It may be both! All true purposes are worthy. The important thing is to discover what is true for *you*.

I don't know exactly how we come to have our purpose. Did we choose it before this life (my personal belief)? Is it a result of our upbringing? Do our genetics steer us toward certain preferences? Is it some combination of these, or something else entirely? Regardless of where our purpose originates, I know everyone has one and that it is essential to a fulfilled life. So let's get inspired with a real purpose, shared by one of my students: "To be a channel of source's beauty, love, and peace as purely and clearly as I in my heart can be."

Finding My Purpose, My Creative Flame

How did I find my purpose? Over years of writing my bio for concert programs, a theme revealed itself to me (the *how* of which you'll learn in step one). This golden thread wove together everything I do, feel, and believe in. I realized this thread was my message to myself, others, and the world. It was my purpose! I was instantly energized: *Could this be the same for others? If they recognized their true purpose, would things align for them as well?*

Let me share my purpose with you so that you have an example to consider:

My purpose is to return to my true self. Living my true self allows me to shine my light on all I encounter. In a life-affirming circle, those I meet are empowered to be their true selves, lighting my life in turn.

Decades of teaching piano and harp have proved to me that everyone has a purpose. In my studio I often worked with up to fifty students a week. Music lessons being voluntary, my job was to keep the student motivated. Week in and week out, it was up to me to help the student stay in touch with why music mattered to them. If it didn't matter, why bother? After all, we have to feel something is relevant to our life in order for us to feel like making effort toward it.

Whether my student was five or eighty-five, my question to them was the same: What do *you* want to play? When my student tapped into their heart's desire, something powerful and eternal entered the room. And then I would go deeper, asking, "And what does your chosen song mean to *you*?" The emotional floodgates would open, and clues to their purpose flowed. Feelings are feelings, from the smallest children to seasoned seniors. The greatest beauty: when each person listened to their heart, their purpose spoke directly to them.

Counsel in the heart of man is like deep water;
but a man of understanding will draw it out.

— Proverbs 20:5

Guided by each student's heart wisdom, we pieced their purpose together over time. Our lessons transformed into a playground of joy, discovery, learning, and growth. This was and is the secret to my teaching success. And it is now the open secret to your creative success: *to live your purpose.*

For you *do* have a purpose. You might have forgotten it, denied it, or kept it secret from prying eyes. It hasn't gone away, though. It can't be destroyed, even though it may be buried under years of dust and grime. Let the cleansing fire of your eternal flame shine!

Why Your Purpose Is the First Step on Your Creative Path

The beginning in every task is the chief thing.

— PLATO

When you know your purpose, you can make clear decisions about what projects to take on, how to practice, who to collaborate with, and myriad other creative choices. I notice that creatives often set goals based on other people's desires and opinions rather than on their own hearts. I've done this frequently myself, and it usually leads to me feeling backed into a gloomy corner, stressed and unenthusiastic. Has this happened to you?

Setting goals without knowing your purpose is like taking a shot in the dark. It's unlikely you'll hit a target you really care about. When you know your purpose, your vision sharpens and your aim grows ever true. You can then set intentional goals that motivate you, body, mind, and spirit. And over time you gain skill at all this, setting ever more aligned and exciting goals.

If we don't know our purpose and consequently set random goals, creating a practice plan for these haphazard goals collapses into a pileup of frustration and demotivation. If this occurs, integration (step four) can't happen. Learning and creativity screech to a halt. Fulfillment (step five) becomes impossible.

Adhering to your purpose may sound like a lifelong quest. In a way it is, because you'll always be growing if you live an engaged life. That said, you already possess a jewel-strong purpose (even though it hasn't been articulated yet; sit tight!), as worthy now as it will be years from now. The sooner you identify it, the sooner you will live your most engaged life. And with that, another real purpose to fire you up: *To bear witness and speak.*

Internal vs. External Motivation: Fire Up with Joy

Purpose is fired by *internal* motivation because your purpose comes from within you. How can you tell if you are being driven by internal versus external motivation? Here is the litmus test: if you act because you *have to*, external motivation rules. If you find yourself saying a lot of "I shoulds" or "I have tos" or spending time measuring yourself or your art against others, then external motivation is smothering your light. No matter how worthy that "have to" is, if your heart is not leading, you're not in alignment with your purpose.

On top of that, the "should army," as I like to call that finger-wagging band of enforcers, often doesn't actually exist. The person who cares most about you being creative is *you*. Those who truly love us will love us regardless of what we create. If we hope to be motivated long-term by others rather than ourselves, we'll either burn everyone out with our expectations and/or find ourselves disappointed that no one is "making" us act.

Aristotle understood the power of internal motivation: "Happiness depends upon ourselves," he said, and taught that "happiness is the ultimate end and purpose of human existence." Heeding Aristotle's charge to cultivate our internal happiness, embedded in everything we do here on our Bright Way is another great secret to creativity: *joy*.

Joy is the fiery motivator on our creative journey, a clear expression of love energy. The word *joy* comes from the root *gau*, which in Greek has come to mean "to rejoice" and in Middle Irish translates to "noble." When we rejoice, we connect to the energy of love in gratitude, a noble thing. Joy embodies our most elevated qualities: love, gratitude, and dignity.

If you ever become lost on your creative journey, tap into joy — no matter how tiny; it might simply be a beam of light across your bedspread — to reignite your higher consciousness and imagination. Reclaim your right to exist by connecting to your inherent nobility, the dignity that is yours simply because you *are*. Draw on this joyous energy, any place, any moment. We'll be cultivating this ability throughout our journey.

Many of our institutions, from schools to the media, tell us that only the external (people, places, products, prizes) can grant us happiness. But over time, lack of internal motivation becomes harrowing and confusing. We rebel, we chafe, yet we have nowhere to turn. Excuses and resistance rise. Things we loved, such as writing, dancing, practicing yoga, making music, cooking, become obligations. Mysteriously, we seem to fall out of love with what once meant so much to us, neglecting what used to give us joy and energy. Where did the magic go?

Aligning with your purpose will rekindle your internal motivation. Does this sound incredibly simple? It is! Constant suffering is not our natural state. Ongoing strife is not life affirmation. We are here to create, to reflect the glory of life source.

> Ongoing strife is not life affirmation. We are here to create, to reflect the glory of life source.

Shinichi Suzuki, whose Suzuki Method has produced countless virtuosos, said, "Teaching music is not my main purpose. I want to make good citizens, noble human beings." His striking external results mean that we're mostly aware of the tremendous feats his method achieves. Yet Suzuki confirms that these astonishing achievements are side effects, not the aim. How did he do this? By leading with the heart: "Where the love is deep, much will be accomplished."

Focusing on joy is not a feel-good strategy or a consolation prize for those who can't handle the rigor of practice. On the contrary, engaging joyfully brings outstanding results. Suzuki, who mostly worked with children, stated, "I firmly believe that any child can become superior, and my confidence has never been betrayed" — this from the man who lived to ninety-nine and affected the lives of millions to date, and counting. In working with students of all ages, I have experienced the same thing: that *anyone can create meaningfully if they joyfully engage.*

Life continually throws us challenges, and these aren't going to cease in this great school of life. Can we marshal the energy to persevere joy-fully? When you're in touch with your true self via your pur-pose, you fire up with universal energy, the most potent fuel available. Universal energy is growth; it is ever-expanding, vibrating life force. Ultimately, life force energy is love. And when your true self connects to this source, synergy spirals out, creating a more loving world. Have you heard the phrase "feel-ing at one with the universe"? That's what we're talking about! This real purpose captures it succinctly: "Bliss."

> Anyone can create meaningfully if they joyfully engage.

BRIGHT WAY ACTIVITY
Burning Away Your Burdens

What external expectations have held you back from reconnecting with your true purpose? Write your answers on a slip of paper. Hold on to this piece of paper for the day. Meditate on it. You might even find that your pocket feels heavier because of the psychic load it bears. Tonight, in a safe, well-ventilated area, light a candle — or a fire in your hearth or fire-pit — and burn that slip of paper. Revel in the burning away of burdens you have outgrown. Celebrate the return of your light.

Cultivating Self-Trust: Burning Barriers

In order to access our purpose, we need to burn through the hard, defensive shell of protection that we all present to the world. Once we melt that shell, we directly access the beauty, creativity, and divinity within us.

Let's name our most formidable shield: ego. Your ego, that most human of entities, is designed to protect you, and rightly so. Being totally open and vul-nerable at all times would be overwhelming. The ego also gives us valuable grist for creative growth — we're humans for a reason, after all! The shadow side, though, is that the ego can overstep its role, making us fearful to take risks, even small ones. This happens to all of us. It is not a shameful thing that we are going to judge. Rather, it is something we're going to learn to manage.

Your ego is the voice that tells you, "Don't do that! You'll look silly! You'll get hurt! So-and-so will get annoyed!" This negative self-talk loop sets huge roadblocks in our path, most impressively, fear. Be alert. Notice how many times a day you hear negative self-talk popping up. Catch it when it happens, and disarm it by not playing its game. Scorch the frame negative self-talk is attempting to squeeze you into: "Why would doing that thing make me look silly? To whom? *And so what, anyway?*" Replace all negative self-talk with prepared affirmations, such as:

> *What I say and do matters to me, my soul, and the world.*
> *I am here for a reason: I trust and move forward with hope on my journey.*
> *Life is for living. It is my birthright to pursue and experience joy.*
> *Living creatively is a journey: I focus on experiences rather than destinations, process rather than products.*
> *Who's best at being me? Me! I win!*

Courage is the antidote to fear. Affirmations build courage through positive self-talk, even and especially when you're in fear's grip. When we're afraid, it's hard to think straight, so have your personal list of affirmations ready. Engulf negative self-talk with courageous affirmations, rewiring your mind and body for positivity (your spirit already being a beacon of positivity!).

Your thoughts create your reality. Negative thoughts destroy your courage. The effect on your entire being is devastating. Affirmations may seem puny, even silly in the face of big problems. Yet I've been privy to the most appalling things people say to themselves in private. I've heard students shout at themselves, "You're so stupid" and worse as they play in front of me. If that's what they say out loud, can you imagine what they're saying inside? What must that add up to over time? Make no mistake: your back-pocket affirmations cache is essential. As far back as imperial Rome, Stoic philosopher Emperor Marcus Aurelius understood the power of self-talk: "The things you think about determine the quality of your mind. Your soul takes on the color of your thoughts."

BRIGHT WAY ACTIVITY
Create Your Affirmations

Create three affirmations for yourself and write them in your Bright Way Diary. You might also want to screen-save them or place them anywhere else you'll see multiple times a day. Write your affirmations in completely positive language, such as "I confidently create" rather than "I'm trying to stop being unconfident about creating." Use words that hold great emotional meaning for you, words that touch your heart and soul. Keep your affirmations private for now, so that you can form an intimate relationship with them without feeling like external eyes are privy to them. Update your affirmations as needed as you grow on this journey.

Circulating the Sacred Fire: Start with Your Spark

In self-trust, we gain the courage to dare to be vulnerable, opening the door to sharing ourselves authentically. We expose our full-spectrum human experience, in all its highs, lows, triumphs, and catastrophes. Inviting others in to connect and sincerely hear us, we open the door to hearing them in turn. The flow of connection circulates. Creativity expands outward and reflects back again, sustaining itself. On this journey you are cycling back and forth between the external and internal, discovering that we exist in a state of "interbeing," as Buddhist monk Thich Nhat Hanh calls it.

Yet the initiatory spark, the recognition of your flame, must once again originate from inside you. This is your spirit being made manifest in our world through *your* unique purpose. Learning to trust yourself is one of the greatest creative gifts you will give yourself. If you're not there yet, please don't get frustrated or beat yourself up about it. Cultivating self-trust is a radical act in today's world. Take one small step at a time. Here are my five favorite guidelines to help you get started:

1. **Conduct a personal environmental assessment.** Are the people surrounding you supportive? If not, it's time to cultivate your community of creative allies. These allies give you support, feedback, and inspiration. Many of humanity's most influential artistic developments happened in community, as we'll discover in Bright Way step five. Seek out local groups of writers, artists, chefs, parents — whomever resonates with your purpose. Online communities complement local allies and may even be your entire support network in some circumstances. You need and deserve a supportive environment in order for your creativity to flourish.

2. **Honor your promises to yourself.** Start right here: make a promise to yourself to follow through on your journey. Trust that you are on the right path. Know that you're doing something wonderful for yourself.

3. **Reframe negative self-talk.** Because it is such an important topic, I offer you an additional technique in handling the beast that is negative self-talk. When it rears its ugly head, neutralize it with the "but technique." Saying "but" negates whatever comes before it. If negative self-talk says: "I can't play fluently, I'm hopeless and clunky," your reframe is: "I can't play fluently right now, *but* I'm learning technique and playing with greater flow every day." The sting of the first statement is soothed and then reoriented via a positive plan of action, all in one fell swoop. If you don't find the word *but* helpful, try *and* or *yet*.

4. **Listen to your body.** Your body is an early warning system for whether you are in alignment with your true purpose. Listen to it. Does your heart feel expansive or constricted? Does your stomach leap with excitement or feel sick with dread? Do your lips form an involuntary smile, or are they pursed in worry? Heed your five senses: they're hardwired for truth.

5. **Get to know your sixth sense: intuition.** As you live deeper through your five senses, another sense mysteriously emerges. This is your sixth sense, intuition. Everyone has intuition, although we're often

taught to ignore, deny, or silence it. You know your intuition is active when insights seem to pop into your mind out of nowhere. You "know" certain things. This reality beyond your five senses is a major source of your magic.

BRIGHT WAY ACTIVITY
Pick a Positive Habit

Journeys are made up of many little footfalls. As you build self-trust, try this simple technique: pick a tiny, positive habit you'd like to create, and commit to following through on it daily. In fulfilling this commitment, you allow your self-trust to grow. The documented benefits are astonishing, especially given how small this step may seem.

This idea was furthered by the colorfully named B. J. Fogg, who recommends that whatever you pick as your habit last for fewer than thirty seconds, require some effort, and be linked to a trigger. Some examples are: take a few deep breaths at stoplights, pause before opening your first day's email to remember one thing you're grateful for, take a stretch when you get up from your work chair. As you complete your habit day after day, you come to believe in your ability to follow through. And since creativity is an ongoing journey, follow-through — also known as action — is something we want to cultivate as second nature.

Your Step One Essential Element: Inspiration (Fire) △

It's time to deepen our relationship with the fire of inspiration. Your purpose fuels your entire creative journey. In turn, the essential element of inspiration is your creative fire. You can motivate yourself with threats in the form of harsh deadlines and embarrassing consequences. Being fear-based, these tactics fail long-term, drying up your enthusiasm and, in a worst-case scenario, making you quit. Instead, motivate yourself by cultivating your inspiration.

Growing your inspiration consciously may sound like a contradiction — doesn't inspiration just strike when it feels like it? Look back on the histories of the great artists: they went to great and daily lengths to tend their inspirational fire. They did not leave inspiration up to chance. They sent out gorgeous invitations to the muse by setting the inspiration table lavishly. We'll uncover many ways to grow your inspiration on our journey together. As an example, consider the inspirational power that these invocations contain:

In the *Odyssey*, Homer invokes his muse:

Tell me, O Muse, of the man of many devices, who wandered full many ways after he had sacked the sacred citadel of Troy....
    Of these things, goddess, daughter of Zeus, beginning where thou wilt, tell thou even unto us.

The hymn "Veni Sancte Spiritus," sometimes called the Golden Sequence, is prescribed in the Roman Catholic liturgy to be sung by monks and nuns at the start of the day for purity in all work, creative and otherwise:

Come, Holy Spirit, send forth the heavenly radiance of your light.
Come, father of the poor, come, giver of gifts, come, light of the heart.
Greatest comforter, sweet guest of the soul, sweet consolation.
In labor, rest, in heat, temperance, in tears, solace.
O most blessed light, fill the inmost heart of your faithful.
Without your spirit, there is nothing in man, nothing that is not harmful.
Cleanse that which is unclean, water that which is dry,
heal that which is wounded.
Bend that which is inflexible, fire that which is chilled,
correct what goes astray.
Give to your faithful, those who trust in you,
the sevenfold gifts [wisdom, understanding, counsel, fortitude,
knowledge, piety, and reverence of God].
Grant the reward of virtue, grant the deliverance of salvation, grant eternal joy.

And taking cues from a more Earth-based philosophy:

Welcome, fire of my inspiration,
Water of my flowing emotions,
Air of my free thought,
Earth of my grounding support,
Spirit of my soul and beloveds,
Welcome, all!

BRIGHT WAY ACTIVITY
Craft Your Invocation

Craft your own invocation to inspiration. Remember your allies. Can you call on them to bless your work? Does a memory of a grandparent bring inspiration and joy? Does your spiritual path give you cues for invocations? Do the energies of nature inspire you? Does invoking your creative heroes connect you to inspiring lineage? Write your invocation ideas in your Bright Way Diary. Use your invocation before each creative session. Notice how it works for you, and adjust as needed. You might even consider starting each day with your invocation.

One of the most effective ways to stoke your inspiration is to notice what moves you. What do you find beautiful? What is meaningful to you? What makes you feel curious? Follow these signs. They are what resonate with you. Spend time with these creativity clues, unapologetically, even when you can't quite understand their meaning or value at the moment.

As you gravitate toward what resonates with you,

> As you gravitate toward what resonates with you, you get closer to your personal style. You gain the confidence to spend time on what you love.

you get closer to your personal style. You gain the confidence to spend time on what you love. I've seen this happen when harpists finally realize they love to play slow and magnificent Gregorian chants rather than feeling obliged to keep up with the fiddlers at the local Celtic session. Suddenly a galaxy of creative possibility opens to them. I've seen people start arranging, improvising, and composing, as they become so deeply in contact with their style that they feel the need to express it on their own terms.

BRIGHT WAY ACTIVITY
What Moves You?

As you go about your day, notice what moves you emotionally. Which sounds move you? What is an evocative taste to you? What is a mind-expanding visual to you? Which smells trigger memories? Which textures give you comfort? Log your reflections in your Bright Way Diary, coming back to them whenever you need a jolt of inspiration. Keep adding to your inspiration list as time goes on.

Protect and Activate with Love

We're doing deep work together, so let's ensure that you are protected. I know how vulnerable this work feels and what it can open up. I want you to feel safe.

Your best protection is the energy of love. So ask for blessings on your journey from your allies, nature, guides, God (however you conceive of God), your ancestors, the energies that make you feel safest and most beloved.

You might say something like:

> *Thank you to my beloved protector. I feel love and gratitude for you. Please bless and guide my work for the highest good, for myself and all those around me.*
> *I trust my journey and sense loving support right here with me. Thank you for your presence. I feel your arms around me and your smile warming me.*

I sense my strength, fueled by the Earth's power. Dear Earth, please keep filling me with life-affirming energy so that I can manifest my greatest truth into the world.

BRIGHT WAY ACTIVITY
Using a Protection Mantra

Create your own protection prayer or mantra, using language and imagery that are most natural for you. Write this in your Bright Way Diary. Use this prayer/mantra whenever you're about to embark on deep, heart-opening work. Or at any other time! You can never go wrong when you call on the power of love.

In this state of beloved protection, it's now time to connect deeply with your core self, via the process of harmonizing with yourself.

Harmonize with Yourself: Connect to Your Center

Many tools across cultures and time foster centering, meditation being a well-known example. If I were only allowed to teach one thing, it would be centering. It's that important!

Speaking as a musician, when all aspects of a song flow together, they are in harmony. In harmony, music feels greater than the sum of its visible parts. Similarly, by harmonizing with yourself — the Bright Way version of centering — you connect to your true self, the self beyond mind and body, the self that is bigger than any of us can imagine. This feeling of true connection with your core self is what centering allows.

You can practice harmonizing with yourself as many times a day as you like: at your desk, at work, before you begin engaging with your art form. As with any skill, the more you practice, the better you will get at it. Initially, it may take time to feel fully centered. Eventually, centering will become a habit you can trigger in a flash. Let's begin. Close your eyes and then follow these actions:

- **FOCUS on this moment.** Let the outside world recede. Know that you are safe and complete. You might enjoy visualizing a meaningful symbol, perhaps a place, person, or thing you love unconditionally. This infuses you with the energy of "love and allowing" rather than "effort and thinking."
- **CONNECT with your heart,** feeling its loving energy expand out like a balloon, infinitely. Bathe in this energy and warmth. Feel gratitude for this infinite resource; its energy is your greatest safety and inspiration.
- **BREATHE,** right down into your belly. Gently fill your lungs to capacity, allowing their lower reaches to expand. Breathe calmly and fully, in through your nose, if possible, and out whatever way feels right for you at this moment. Take your time. Sense how natural it is for you to breathe. Be here in this moment.
- **Release any bodily tension so that you can OPEN up.** Breathe spaciousness into any tight spots. Scan from the crown of your head down to your toes (or the other way round, if you prefer) for opportunities to open further. You might enjoy deliberately yawning: opening and closing your jaw quiets emotional chatter. Perhaps you start to feel warmer. Other people report feeling cooler, or that time seems to slow. Everyone is different. Get to know your body's responses.
- **Last, EMBODY this moment with all your senses.** Touch, hear, taste, smell, and see this moment. You may feel tingly with sensation, alive and available. You might feel something completely different — that's fine! Encode your sensation of total embodiment and presence into your consciousness by tapping gently between your eyebrows. Similar to the effects of acupuncture and acupressure, this small action stimulates both the pineal gland and the amygdala — producers of melatonin and sometimes thought to be the seat of our soul — which in turn activates the pituitary gland and hypothalamus, stimulating growth and reprogramming you for positivity. (This technique is used in many arenas, from ancient Chinese medicine to treating PTSD survivors today.)

To sum up, below is a diagram of the harmonizing process. You might enjoy tracing each stage with your finger, recalling the sensation of each as an instant review exercise:

Figure 7. The Stages of Harmonizing with Yourself

The portal is open. You are ready to reveal your purpose.

Scribe Your Purpose

Get out your Bright Way Diary and a writing utensil. Writing by hand has a magical way of making things real. You engage physically with your thoughts. You make your mark, literally. Writing is commitment. There's no delete button, which allows you to be more honest with yourself. (This can feel pretty bracing at times!) What's more, handwriting recalls your first childhood scribbling, reclaiming beginner's mind (explored further in Bright Way step two) and its wide-open horizons.

Writing by hand slows you down so that you can savor the moment. It's an invitation to go deeper. Because it is more private than typing on a device, its hallmarks are focus and rawness. Handwriting is intimate: your personality and state of mind are reflected in your unique hand. (Sidenote: I used to do handwriting analysis for fun, and it's uncanny how revealing it can be!) You might even sense handwriting as incantation: in the act of writing, you enter sacred space, casting *your* wondrous spell.

Now recall and write down your earliest memories of being drawn to your art, and by art I mean whatever creative endeavor matters to you. Let imagery and feelings flow freely. Whatever comes to mind, write it down immediately. Let go of judgment and logic. You'll have ample opportunity to organize everything in our later Bright Way steps. Stay harmonized with yourself. "Stream of consciousness" and "for my eyes only" are your mantras here, sidestepping concerns about grammar, spelling, or penmanship.

Memory is the scribe of the soul.

— Aristotle

If you get stuck or feel apprehensive, here are some prompts to help you:

- **Ask yourself:** "What attracted me to my art in the first place? What feelings did it give me?" How did you feel before you knew what you know now about your art? Go for pure, first-encounter feelings. Be specific and vivid, using all your senses.
- **Recall details:** "Where was I when I was first inspired? What was happening around me? Who was there?" Describe these details down to the smallest particulars; gems of insight are often buried within.
- **Follow up with multiple "whys":** "I was attracted to my art because it seemed exciting. Why?" Answer, and then follow up with another "why?" I've found that people are often astounded at the power and relevance of what gets unearthed when they persist in asking themselves the whys behind the why.

If you have no specific creative endeavor in mind, that's okay. Focus instead on your earliest memories of something you *loved* doing, especially something you enjoyed so much that you got lost in time. Losing track of time is a sure sign that you're engaged in magic.

Were you making music? Playing on a beach? Running up a mountain?

Inventing imaginary worlds with your friends (perhaps with imaginary friends)? Keith, our computer scientist and artist, recalls: "My earliest and innermost example of enjoying the creative moment is when I would get lost in drawing or coloring as a child. Time would cease to exist, and I would be in a sunny spot on the floor or at the table, absorbed in what I was doing."

What do your memories sound like? What tastes do they evoke? What do they look like? What colors are emerging? What smells are conjured up by your memories? How do they feel to the touch? We're born with synesthesia yet forget this synergetic ability over time. Synesthesia is the cross-fertilization of senses, where you might experience a sound as having a particular color or a taste having a certain sound. Synesthesia stokes inspiration and improves our learning abilities. Fiction writer and editor Jessica Hatch elaborates on how synesthesia also reconnects us to our earliest selves: "There are so many sophisticated pastimes that use synesthetic language (e.g., wine tasting involving taste, mouth feel, nose, and vision). It would make sense that we hold such things in high regard because we're all trying to get back to our most innocent and synesthetic state."

All this might feel odd or even outrageous at first. Connect with your heart energy to bypass ego chatter and other censors. Being able to tolerate feeling silly is such an underrated creative skill. Have fun with this!

If your initial feelings or images are vague or scattered, that's fine, too. It might take a few attempts to get into the zone. Give your feelings and memories time and space to unfold. Take your time. This isn't a race or a competition. Have faith that you *will* uncover your answers. Keep reharmonizing with yourself, engaging your five senses so that your sixth sense strengthens.

Remember, in the privacy of your protected sacred workspace (which you'll explore in Bright Way step four), you are safe to roam. If you find yourself getting emotional, that is a great sign. Long-hidden feelings are being liberated, long-buried treasure unearthed. Conversely, squashed feelings are a major source of disease and despair. Let go of them, and invite the healing in.

Remember to contact your allies if you need extra assistance during any part of this process. As you work through issues and detox, it can be rough. Be compassionate with yourself. Trust that your honesty has great value for you and others. Much creativity comes from facing our shadows. You are a creative alchemist, transmuting lead into gold.

And with that, it's time for a break, don't you feel?

BRIGHT WAY BREAK
Relax and Replenish

A sustainable system cycles between active and receptive states; our Bright Way Breaks put us in receptive mode. You've done much deep work already on the way to finding your purpose. Reward yourself with a cup of tea, a stroll, something fun to read, a chat with a friend, some yoga poses, a meditation app, whatever makes you feel relaxed and happy.

When you feel replenished, please review what you did in your Bright Way Diary. Taking note of how your Bright Way Break worked for you builds a repository of refreshing actions you can refer to whenever you need a break. Often, when we're ready for a break, the last thing we want to do is try to make a bunch of decisions!

Trust that all is "unfolding as it should," as Max Ehrmann put it in his "Desiderata." You don't need to force anything, rush ahead, or worry whether or not you're doing things right. There's no right or wrong here. Start getting to know your own pace and what works best for you. This may be the first time you're allowing yourself this luxury. Enjoy it! You're setting the stage for your weeks, months, and even years ahead. Reflect the spirit you want to live, inside and out. Be the change you want to see.

Why It's Key to Write Your Purpose Down

I've noticed that when people write down their purpose rather than just think about it in their heads, their results are strikingly more powerful. Screenwriter Dave Mahony shares his experience:

"I was tempted not to write my creative purpose down. I thought about it, I mused about it, I even talked about it. Wasn't that enough? But it was only when I wrote it down that the magic really happened.

1. It was on the paper looking back at me. I had brought it into material form. It was like seeing myself in the mirror, naked. It was scary and took courage. But now that I could see it, I could hold myself accountable to it. And it to me.

2. Writing the words made my purpose specific. Just because I'd thought about something didn't mean I'd committed myself to truly articulating it. Like a location on a map or a star in the sky, the specificity matters.

3. The physical act reconditioned the creative act itself. By writing it down, I 're-created' my creative process in literal form. After all those years of worry and stuckness and timidity, I reprogrammed those neural pathways to my true intention. It was like exorcising a ghost!

    Once it was written down, once I'd written it, I could see how fear had held me back from expressing it. Fear of it not being enough or good enough…how I wasn't enough. It was that same fear that had kept me from expressing my authentic creative self all along!"

I strongly urge you to take a stand for your creative self and commit to writing your purpose, as described in this Bright Way step's exercises. I've seen people think and talk diligently about their purpose for years, only to make a big breakthrough immediately when they finally wrote it down. Yes, it takes more effort to write rather than just think, but I can't deny the superior results I've witnessed when people write down their purpose. I don't want you to shortchange yourself. Scribe with joy!

Reveal the Essence of Your Memories

You now have a written collection of memories, feelings, images, and thoughts. These contain the essence of your purpose. Let's reveal this essence through these actions:

Pick out themes. Identify words, phrases, images, and statements that show up consistently. Collate them onto a separate page in your Bright Way Diary. As patterns emerge, notice and name them. These patterns hold your themes. Perhaps you're noticing themes of healing, sharing knowledge, love, beauty, exploration, celebrating heritage, reconnecting with the Earth, empowerment, spirituality, or the metaphysical. At this point, any theme is possible! Note them all.

Speak your themes out loud. Just as writing by hand is more evocative than typing, saying things out loud is more powerful than simply hearing them in your head. When you speak, you commit. Speaking is a visceral experience involving all your senses. Your body and spirit react to your spoken words, and this is in itself diagnostic. How are your body and spirit resonating? Notice specifics. Does your heart vibrate in agreement with the words you are saying, or does it constrict in dissonance? Does your soul expand with your words or tighten? Are you stumbling over your words, or are you articulating confidently? These sensations tell you which themes truly align with your soul. Notice which themes have most resonance for you.

Refine your most resonant themes into sentences. Play with word placement until these statements ring true. Ideally, your purpose can be crystallized into one to three sentences (sometimes even one word!) for easy recall.

Here are some additional examples of purposes from real Bright Way practitioners to spark your imagination:

> *I play the harp to find my way home, to experience delight, and to attune myself to the Mystery.*
>
> *To discover what the world, the universe, and life is all about and what I can do with it.*
>
> *To write for the One so the Many can hear.*

Three Tips for Creating a Powerful Purpose

It's been my privilege to help hundreds of creative souls identify their purpose. I've encountered three common pitfalls during this process. Here are my favorite tips for handling these issues with ease:

1. **Make sure your purpose focuses on *you*.** If your purpose reads something like *I create to make others joyful,* then reframe it. It's easy for us, when discerning our noble purposes, to get sidetracked into trying to please others and to conform to external expectations. Take charge and stand center stage. Consider this alternative: *I create to bring joy to myself, thereby spreading joy to others in turn.*

   Here are more reframed examples to help you keep your purpose focused on *you:*

   I paint to inspire others.
   I paint to connect directly to my inspiration and feel alive. In doing this, I inspire others to do the same.
   I dance to show that moving and enjoying your body can happen at any age.
   I dance to feel alive, healthy, and vital. In doing so, I help empower others to feel alive, healthy, and vital.

   Lay aside worries about being selfish. Remember As Above, So Below? Here's an amazing phenomenon I've noticed: when you align with your purpose, the momentum of your emotional investment brings people along with you. When I perform in harmony with myself, the audience comes with me far more than if I were *trying* to get them to feel something in particular. The deeper I am in my purpose, the more it broadcasts effortlessly. Sometimes audience members even tell me they saw the exact image that I had in my mind's (soul's?) eye while playing. Focus on your purpose, and others will benefit.

   > The deeper I am in my purpose, the more it broadcasts effortlessly.

2. **Make sure your true purpose is feelings-based, not facts-based.** Purpose needs emotional charge to be compelling enough to fuel your creative journey. If your statement reads *My purpose is to improve my technique so that I can play with flow,* save it for the facts-based

practicum plan in Bright Way step three. Instead, empower your purpose to be visceral, emotional, and values driven. Consider: *My purpose is to flow in my art so that I feel in flow with life.*

Here's another instance of a purpose reframed viscerally:

My purpose is to write for two hours a day.
My purpose is to discover my deepest, truest self through a committed writing practice so that I can live in devoted love.

3. **Frame your purpose in positive language.** "Don't think of an elephant!" instantly brings a pachyderm to mind. Our brains have a funny way of focusing on the negative, even when we intend the opposite. Choose positive language for your purpose, for example: *As a writer, my purpose is to ~~never sate~~ stoke my curiosity and to always learn new things about the world around me.* A small tweak lights this purpose up with sunny energy!

Finally, here are some additional examples of real purposes from my students to inspire you further:

To celebrate my heritage and feel strengthened by its wisdom.
To be a clear channel of light.
To feel connected and therefore connect with others.

BRIGHT WAY ACTIVITY
Display Your Purpose!

Write your purpose on a beautiful sheet of paper or a sticky note. Display it prominently. Put it in places where you will read it regularly. Your purpose is a grand thing that deserves pride of place. Beside your bed, in your bathroom, in your wallet, on your fridge, as a screensaver: these are all ideal spots.

Completing Step One: Commit to Your Purpose

You now have a bright, working version of your purpose in the form of approximately one to three emotion-packed sentences that thrill you to speak aloud. If words aren't your favored medium for this, you might instead have a distinct symbol, sound, or sensation representing your purpose. If your purpose isn't polished yet, that's fine! We all refine over time as we grow. I've seen many a purpose morph and develop. That said, I've never seen anyone contradict what they came up with initially, so you are most certainly on the right track.

The important thing now is to commit to your purpose. Allow it to infuse your day, your actions, your choices, your consciousness. You'll start feeling and responding to stimuli, requests, and challenges from the higher consciousness your purpose embodies. Your joy will increase, as will your resilience. Synchronicities will abound, patterns will reveal themselves more readily, opportunities will arise, and connections will become deeper and more fulfilling. By identifying your purpose, you more easily let go of things that don't support it. Life becomes very magical from here on out!

Now let's get your magic flowing by setting your intentions — our Bright Way version of goals — from this place of purpose. These are going to be intentions like you've never set before, goals with heart and soul. Intentions that are 100 percent in alignment with your purpose. These intentions excite you and keep you motivated over the long term because they reflect your purpose.

It's time to get intentional in step two!

Step Two:
Set Your Intentions

Pour Heart and Soul into Your Purpose

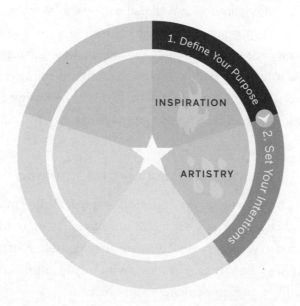

Your purpose needs a container. It's easy to feel swamped by the myriad choices and possibilities around us. Choosing what to do with your purpose can be anxiety provoking, even when the dreaming feels exciting.

When it comes to setting goals, do you worry about making the wrong choice or starting down the wrong path? Does this worry paralyze you and keep you from acting at all? Maybe you fear missing out on opportunities, so you undertake my own personal pitfall: striking out in twenty directions simultaneously? How about Shiny Object Syndrome, in which every new idea seems to be the best thing ever? Or perhaps you simply can't see ahead without a target?

Take a breath, and rest easy. When you're guided by your purpose, you can't go wrong.

> When you're guided by your purpose, you can't go wrong.

How is this possible? Well, as you know, your purpose reflects your true self, which is tapped into ultimate wisdom. It can't lead you astray. Think of your purpose not as a linear path forward but as the compass you use to navigate any and all paths forward. Many roads lead to your truth, not just one. Trust yourself. I see astonishing ideas and dreams emerge when people, myself included, trust their purpose enough to follow it through with intention. And that is the key: rather than setting end-oriented goals, on the Bright Way you will be setting intentions. Let's dive into the reasons and mindset behind this approach.

Flowing into Emotion and Intuition

Water is our natural element for this step, representing emotion, intuition, dreams, flow, and change. You'll set intentions based on these life-giving qualities, along with artistry, our essential element for this step. Facts and figures can wait until Bright Way step three. For now, swim in your intuition, allowing new depths of possibility and expression to widen for you.

Your alchemical operation has advanced to *dissolution*. Metaphorically, we place the remaining ashes from fiery calcination into a water-filled container. We allow them to float free; the dross will get strained off, and whatever dissolves in total integration shall be retained. Likewise, you'll allow your purpose to float in an emotion-honoring state, and only those intentions that merge with your purpose shall remain.

BRIGHT WAY ACTIVITY
Invoke Water ▽

Turn to the diagram at the start of this chapter. Color in the step two/ artistry pie piece, using whatever color invokes water for you. Feel yourself flow with energy as you do this meditation. If you have no color writing utensils, move on to part two of this activity: draw the alchemical symbol for water (▽) inside the pie piece, even spreading out over the page. Feel the sweeping energy of the downward triangle, reflecting the tendency of water to always seek greater depth.

Intentions vs. Traditional Goals

Bright Way intentions are similar to goals, as we usually conceive of them, with these critical differences: intentions are *heart-centered* rather than head-based, and *open-ended* rather than final. Let's dive deeper.

Intentions Are Heart-Centered

One of the first objections I hear from creatives when it comes to setting goals is that they don't want to be fenced in by rules and regimens. I love this bold attitude! It prioritizes heart and soul. It acknowledges the mystery of the creative path, which can't be hemmed in.

Goals have an odd way of becoming opponents rather than allies. In my teaching I have discovered that, over time, students' goals morph into external creatures. It isn't long before these creatures feel hostile. In contrast, intentions, being heart-centered, remained intensely personal and positive. Because of this, intentions stay relevant and emotionally charged for far longer than traditional goals. Intentions have more emotional open space, especially helpful when they take longer to manifest than originally expected, which has happened to us all!

Intentions Are Open-Ended

Another fear I hear is that setting goals is scary because unless we can complete something "perfectly," it's not worth doing. Better not set goals in the first place, since they could lead to stress and disappointment, right?

This is an understandable attitude, and another reason why setting intentions instead of traditional goals often works better. Intentions are open-ended enough to outwit perfectionism. Intentions are flexible — much like water! — and can't be constricted into a mold of perfection. The ineffectiveness of perfectionism has been proven on a practical level, not to mention on the emotional and spiritual levels as well. The eighty-twenty rule shows that 80 percent of our results come from 20 percent of our efforts. In this light, perfectionism is simply a waste of energy! Instead, find your magical 20 percent, and capitalize on that.

The Creative Benefits of Setting Intentions

Now that we've compared intentions to traditional goals, let's focus on how intentions positively impact your creative process. I've seen amazing turnarounds happen for people when they simply reframe their goals as heart-centered intentions, without having to change a single other thing. Let's delve into these creative waters.

Intentions: The Container for Your Creativity

Without a container for your creativity — an intention — chances are your creative urges will remain vague. They will float like clouds, up and away, or spread like a puddle on the ground. Instead, let your urges be channeled into a vigorous river, moving through new places, taking on people and influences, carving new routes, and bringing fresh adventures to you and those you touch.

Take a look at our familiar skill-magic diagram on the next page. Notice the new pole of intention. When you bring your skill and magic together with intention, manifestation gains even more flow.

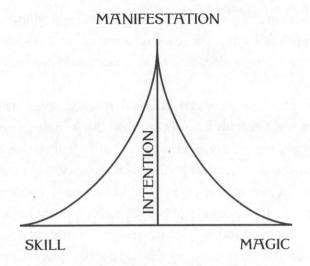

Figure 8. The Pole of Intention

BRIGHT WAY ACTIVITY
The Pole of Intention

Draw the diagram pictured above in your Bright Way Diary. Trace its lines with your fingers and say the words *skill-magic-intention-manifestation* out loud. Feel the integrity the pole of intention now adds to the pyramid. Visualize the wave of manifestation gaining power through intention. What does this pole make you feel? Strong? Clear? Is there a little flutter of excitement? Is it slightly scary? Write down your feelings.

Intentions: Keeping You Present and Available

It's a strange phenomenon that, over time, our minds filter out sounds that aren't part of our language (or languages, if we're lucky enough to speak several). In order to avoid overwhelm, the brain selects for sounds that we hear frequently and literally doesn't register foreign ones. It's as if those sounds never happened. If we cannot perceive the sounds, there is no way for us to produce them.

Similarly, traditional goals can filter out options, inspiration, even feedback. If something doesn't fall within the scope of our goal, we may not notice it. Yet that thing might be the very clue, tool, or idea that could float our creative boat to the next level.

Receiving feedback at every turn is how I reached levels that would have been closed to me had I kept my blinders on. Take, for instance, the day I realized performance anxiety wasn't my enemy but my ally. Before that day, my end-oriented goal had been to vanquish performance anxiety. That goal blinded me to the possibility that performance energy could ever have a positive side. Once I learned that it was all a question of *managing* this phenomenal energy, my anxiety became excitement and my performances became magnetic (and this can happen for you, too!). If I'd stuck to my original goal of conquering performance anxiety, I probably wouldn't be here today writing this book.

Intentions entail present-day awareness rather than future-focus on distant goals. Goals can make us project into the future in such a way that we don't see what's right in front of us. We don't appreciate the journey because we're obsessing over the final result. Intentions keep us here, in the now, in the flow. There's no better place to be!

Intentions: Invitations, Not Orders

The muse thrives when she's invited rather than ordered to arrive. She prefers to be given space to work her magic. She refuses to be controlled. Intentions, being open-ended, provide space for your muse (however you define this inspirational source energy) to collaborate. Magic moves through you in a way that might make others whisper, "Genius!"

When we attempt to control the muse — I want to stress that this is always an attempt, never successful — with orders in the guise of goals, collaborative energy becomes dammed up. Offer your intentions as invitations to your muse so that you can dream, dare, and achieve more than you ever thought possible. This has happened for me, and I'm confident it will for you, too.

BRIGHT WAY ACTIVITY (OR IS IT A BREAK?)
Immerse Yourself

Immerse yourself in water. You might draw a bath, take a shower, dive into the ocean or a nearby lake or river, or, if none of these opportunities is available to you, hold your hand under a running faucet. How does the water feel against your skin? How does it sound when you move a hand or a foot through it, or when you lower your ears beneath its surface? Do you feel energized by the water? Cleansed? Lighter? More present?

Your Step Two Essential Element: Artistry (Water) ▽

We've ignited through the fire of the essential element of inspiration in step one (△). Now we flow with the water of the essential element of artistry in step two (▽).

With your intentions you express your purpose in the world, and with artistry you express in general. High artistry is effective communication. The more artistry you cultivate, the more expression you're capable of. When you focus on your artistry, your expression becomes more visceral, direct, and provocative, always backed up with heart-centered compassion.

Like the natural element of water, artistry is not a fixed entity. Everyone has artistry within. Artistry is an ongoing revelation taking many forms, always morphing and growing. Much as water is essential to life, artistry is essential to your creative expression, a natural and elemental part of you.

> Artistry is essential to your creative expression, a natural and elemental part of you.

The Three Pillars of Artistry

In the course of my work, I have identified three pillars to support artistry, no matter the field. Lean on these pillars now to support new ideas, feelings, and perceptions. Picture these three pillars forming a great tripod upholding the container of your artistry.

Beginner's Mind

Beginner's mind (*shoshin* 初心 is the Zen Buddhist term) is an attitude of wonder, openness, and freshness. Poetically, the literal translation of the Japanese character is "first heart," referring to that first heartfelt response to something new.

Beginner's mind is another iteration of self-trust because we are lowering our shields enough to admit that we don't know everything. We're willing to play, to experiment, to entertain unusual perspectives, to be silly and have fun.

Children are often envied for their ability to pick things up quickly. This ability makes complete sense; after all, children still have beginner's mind. They absorb what they encounter, unfiltered. They don't throw obstacles in their own way or try to shoehorn lessons into familiar categories, as many adults do.

On the Bright Way, you are encouraged to adopt beginner's mind often, because "in the beginner's mind there are many possibilities, in the expert's mind there are few." Beginner's mind opens you up to new experiences and opportunities. Be kind, be willing to take chances and make mistakes, and be spontaneous! Your artistry — and so much else — will flow!

Presence

You must be present in order to be expressive. If we're distracted, our artistic responses diminish. One of the best ways to stay present is to harmonize with yourself before engaging creatively. You'll bring your entire self, body-mind-spirit, to bear. You're all in; feeling, seeing, touching, tasting, smelling, thinking, responding, *being* on all dimensions with your art. Expression springs freely when you are this engaged.

You'll also find that moralistic judgments fade when you are present. Seeing things as good or bad feels intuitively off when we're truly present. Discernment, with its bright spirit of inquiry, fits better. Discernment means we ask: Is this thing working? If so, why? If not, why not? Discernment will be a faithful guide during Bright Way step four, and we'll become familiar with it then. For now, staying present is more than enough and is sure to increase your artistry.

Deep Listening

I think we've all experienced this: you think you're saying one thing, but others hear something else altogether. Since artistry is about expressing with clarity and depth, this is an especially disconcerting situation for creatives. Deep listening, as taught by Thich Nhat Hanh, provides a solution to this problem.

Deep listening happens when you fully absorb what the other person is saying, without debate or attachment to the right- or wrongness of it. Often we perceive only a shadow of what is actually happening inside people, and this can be the case with your creativity, too.

Whatever your creative endeavor, deep listen to it. What do you *really* hear flowing from your pen, your paintbrush, your instrument, your mouth? While presence asks you to be subjective, very first person, deep listening asks for objectivity. Be honest about what you hear or feel, without judgment or agenda for a particular outcome to manifest. This process works wonders for your progress and expression! Deep listen to others as well for inspiration and discernment. How are they expressing? What do you hear that is new or surprising? How are they getting these effects? How can you integrate these deep listening observations into your artistry?

BRIGHT WAY ACTIVITY
The Three Pillars

Write the Three Pillars of Artistry — beginner's mind, presence, and deep listening — in your Bright Way Diary. Plan one way you can lean on each pillar during your next practice session. How can you approach your creativity with the spirit of beginner's mind? For example, next time you engage your art, pretend it's the first time you're encountering it. Feel that wonder and innocence. Next, ask yourself what practices will help you have more presence. Harmonizing with yourself before each practice, for example? And how can you listen deeper to yourself? Perhaps by recording yourself? Jot down all your ideas.

The Seven Stages of Setting Your Intentions

You now know why intentions are preferred over end-oriented traditional goals. Allied with water, the essential element of artistry, and the operation of dissolution, you're free-floating in an intuitive, artistic mindset. It's time to do the alchemical work of dreaming up your first set of intentions in support of your purpose. This process entails seven stages. They cover a great deal of ground: rest assured that strategic Bright Way Breaks will give you resting spots along the way. Let's explore these stages one by one.

1. Find a Quiet Time

Aim for at least twenty minutes of uninterrupted private time. Turn off devices, and limit distractions. If you live or create in a noisy or highly stimulating environment, you may have to retreat to your local library or even just your car. That's fine! The Bright Way is realistic about the interplay between dreams and our real world, between skill and magic. If you find you need to pull over to the side of the road to write your intentions on a yellow legal pad, I see magic afoot there. Some of my best ideas have come to me in rather unromantic locations. I chuckle at the contrast of transcendental ideas scribbled on the back of the gas station receipt.

2. Write Your Purpose in Your Bright Way Diary

Write it down, and then read your purpose out loud. Feel its power fire you up.

3. Harmonize with Yourself

Use your purpose as your focal point this time! Your purpose is your supreme focusing tool, one that will always guide you true. Again, your purpose may contain words, symbols, sounds, sensations, or some combination of these. Since your purpose is so intensely personal, it aligns with your core desires, which will also help with the following stage of harmonizing with yourself.

4. Dive Deeper into Your Desires

Your desires are what your intentions are made of. I believe you already hold powerful desires inside you; it's simply a question of revealing them to yourself. I've found that the best way to reconnect to your desires is to ask yourself to remember them. Questions you might ask yourself may include:

What are my dreams, including ones I may have forgotten or laid aside?
What do I desire to do, anything being possible?
What do I want to create, space and time being no object?
How do I want to feel in my heart of hearts?
What does my dream life look like?
Who and what would I like to be surrounded by?

Let your heart and soul flow free! No dreams are too big or too outrageous. Allow whatever wants to show up to be heard, seen, and felt. Receive the gifts being given to you: they show you the way to manifest your purpose in our world.

Exactly as you did with scribing your purpose (see page 99), write all that is coming to you in your Bright Way Diary. Scribe for your eyes only, unedited. Pour out all your feelings as they bubble up in you.

What would you love to do, see, feel, and create? Keep coming back to your heart-centered desires. Feel them simmer and boil inside you. Your inspiration keeps the heat high, so keep remembering your fiery purpose. You may be startled by the grandeur of your desires. And why not? They are a reflection of your magnificent True Self!

Sidestep the rational, the cerebral. If facts and statistics like "My intention is to practice for two hours a day" percolate up, acknowledge them and lay them aside for the more practical Bright Way step three. Right now, cascade!

STAY HARMONIZED DURING INTENTION SETTING: THE QUESTION OF DESIRE

Consider how water and desire are intimately connected. The Greek goddess Aphrodite, the embodiment of desire (Venus is her Roman counterpart), was born out of the Mediterranean Sea, on Cyprus. Picture her as she emerged, shining and strong, from the foam. Likewise, your desires rise from your deepest emotions, your most intuitive, receptive state. In fact, the root word of *intention* (the Old French *entencion*) means "desire" or "wish."

Desire can feel scary. While Aphrodite was beloved, she was also feared. Maybe, we worry, our desires will lead us astray. Maybe they'll disappoint us. We've all suffered failures and letdowns. But here's the thing: if you're truly harmonized with yourself, genuinely connected to your sacred purpose, your desire is pure. In fact, you *need* the rawness of desire to liberate your heart's song and your soul's calling.

Our desires are often demonized by institutions such as religious organizations, schools, political groups, economic entities, and even family structures. Your true desires embody potent sources of personal energy such as sexuality, self-determination, and innovative ways of doing things. Institutions that are determined to maintain control rather than empower humanity will resist your growing personal agency. By reclaiming your desires, you reclaim your power. Trusting your desires is a courageous act in the root sense of the word — *cor* being Latin for "heart" or "heart-centered." You're choosing love in real time rather than as a lofty ideal that functions only in the best of circumstances.

BRIGHT WAY ACTIVITY
Is Your Desire True or False?

If you're trying to figure out if a desire is true or false, try this technique:

- **Harmonize with yourself** (see page 97 to review this process), *this time with the object of your desire as your focal point.*
- **Check in with your body.** Do you feel a flutter of excitement, butterflies signaling growth and positive opportunity? Or do you feel cold dread? If the former, your desire is most likely true. If cold dread is upon you, leave this desire aside for now. Your body has spoken! Trust it. The more you trust your heart and body, the more accurate and robust your intuition becomes.

Even if fear does temporarily throw you off, consider it an invitation to reharmonize with yourself. This is a golden opportunity. You're teaching yourself how to refocus on your heart and soul in the midst of challenge. This will serve you stoutly during performances and other high-stakes situations. You're building resilience, and it's all good.

BRIGHT WAY BREAK
What Does Your Body Need?

Harmonize with yourself, and ask your body what it most desires. A walk? A nap? A warm drink? A bath? Listen to what your body has to say, and follow through on it. By following through on your intuition, you strengthen it. By honoring your body's messages, you become fluent in your body's language. Candace Pert observes, "Your body is your subconscious mind." Cultivate this potent source of imagination now.

5. Funnel Your Intentions

You have big, wild dreams written down. Now look over your dreams and start picking out themes, just as you did in Bright Way step one. Collate your dreams into themes so that you can discern major patterns. These patterns are your intentions. Write all your findings in your Bright Way Diary. You'll see many examples of real people's intentions on page 123.

Now pick out two to three intentions that you'd like to achieve over the next three months or less. Favor a short time period so that you can track progress easily. Ideally, these intentions can also be easily accomplished, further helping you practice the skill of setting and following through on intentions.

6. Filter Your Intentions through Purpose

Now that you've picked out two or three intentions, filter them once more through your purpose. Do your intentions completely support your purpose? They must align 100 percent in order to be worthy of your time and energy.

Our world offers more fascinating opportunities than we could explore in a thousand lifetimes, let alone one. Daily I have to say no to things and people I would love to teach, learn, or play with. How do I go about this and feel okay with my decisions? By filtering through my purpose! If an intention is not 100 percent in support of my purpose, I lay it gently aside. I might revisit it later, but for right now, if it's not completely in alignment, it must be shelved. There are more than enough intentions in the world that *do* support my purpose totally, and this is true for you, too.

When you know your intentions, it is easier to say no with love. Many of us dread saying no to others — and even to ourselves — because we worry about sounding rude, ungrateful, or uncaring. Yet when we have good reason to decline an invitation, in the form of beautifully crafted intentions backed up by powerful purpose, we have no reason to feel bad. In fact, as we communicate the why of our declination, others will often nod in admiration and even ask how they can help. And no matter the response, you can still feel good for having declined from a place of love rather than anger, frustration, or defensiveness. By graciously laying aside the invitation, you pass it on to someone else who may be a better candidate. Much like a beautiful dress that doesn't suit you, someone else will wear it better. There is no need to toss away or diminish the opportunity. Knowing your intentions, and the grand purpose behind them, offers you this unexpected freedom.

Further, distilling actions through your purpose helps you preserve your energy in all areas of your life. Does taking your child to piano lessons align with your purpose? I could see this being a hearty yes if it means you feel fulfilled rather than drained. Even the most mundane activities can embody meaning, engagement, connection, and therefore creativity. Does buying that new car align with your purpose? If it's not close to a 100 percent yes on your part, consider postponing the purchase. Reserve your energy for what really matters to you.

Know that your purpose ultimately has the aim of uplifting the world. Defending your purpose is an act of love, not selfishness. In fact, you are modeling what it takes to be a creative, engaged person in our world. We need more examples of what this looks like in real life. By living your purpose, you benefit us all!

EXAMPLES OF PURPOSEFUL INTENTIONS
ACHIEVABLE IN THREE MONTHS OR LESS

Jessica, writer and editor:

Purpose. As a writer, my purpose is to stoke my curiosity, to always learn new things about the world around me. I aim to connect with a community, a writing family that bolsters one another, and to smile when my words make them smile.

Intention 1. *To attend more open-mic nights and workshops to benefit my own work and enjoy the work of others.*

Intention 2. *To create a traveling writers' retreat so that I can tend to my twin purposes of community and curiosity.*

Intention 3. *To respect the one-bodied community of myself, too, and find time to write every day or every other day in order to always feel that glow of creating something.*

Janet, harpist and textile artist:

Purpose. I play the harp to find my way home, to experience delight, and to attune myself to the Mystery.

Intention 1. *To deepen my centering practice [harmonizing with yourself]: become more conscious and deliberate about progressively relaxing my body, from toes to head, about visualizing positive outcomes for individual songs based on the character of the song, about imagining that outcome using all my senses, and about circling the energy.*

Intention 2. *To consciously and deliberately develop, understand, and have words to describe my relationships with chords and modes so that I can use them to represent and elicit specific states and feelings.*

Intention 3. *To return to playing at the hospice unit, which I haven't been able to do since I fractured my heel in April. When I return, I will play only music that I love and that manifests my purpose.*

> ## BRIGHT WAY BREAK
> ### *Feel the Connection*

Allow the breadth and expressiveness of the above Bright Way practitioners' words to replenish you. Bask in the knowledge that others are swirling along this journey with you now all over the world. Feel your connection as we all swim in this vast ocean that is the creative life.

7. Filter Your Intentions through the Essential Elements △ ▽ ⟁ ⟱ O

Congratulations, you've come to the final phase in intention setting! Now that you have your worthy intentions, what to do with them? It may seem that there are a million different directions you could take. You're right! The creative path by its very nature means we have infinite choices. How do we move forward, then?

The Five Essential Elements are your dependable guides here. You will now filter each of your intentions through each essential element. By doing this, you gain specific actions to take. Lay aside concerns about how doable each action you come up with is. These will be addressed in Bright Way steps three and four.

As you filter each intention through each essential element, keep track of what you're doing by using the alchemical symbols △ ▽ ⟁ ⟱ O. So for inspiration, put △ in front of each inspiration action statement, and do the same for all the other essential elements, using the corresponding symbols.

If you don't have a lot of ideas related to a particular essential element yet, no problem. After all, we've discussed only inspiration and artistry at any length so far. A teaching mantra I learned from Arabic literature professor Margaret Larkin is: "Move from the known to the unknown, and make it known." Simply start with what you know. Everything is unfolding at its own pace, and you can't miss out on anything on the Bright Way. Hellenistic Neoplatonist philosopher, astronomer, and mathematician Hypatia of Alexandria is said to have agreed:

"Life is an unfoldment, and the further we travel, the more truth we can comprehend. To understand the things that are at our door is the best preparation for understanding those that lie beyond."

In your Bright Way Diary, tapping into your intuition, direct experience, and past wisdom knowledge, write your essential element action items, using your alchemical symbols to keep track of everything. Allow the following filtering examples to help you out during this process.

FILTER THROUGH THE ESSENTIAL ELEMENT OF INSPIRATION (FIRE) △

Ask yourself: *What inspirational needs does my intention have?* Call on fire to spark your inspiration, and use △. What would make you feel more connected to your intention, more enthused about it? Ideas could include looking at great works of art, listening to music, reading about your art, discovering related topics such as the history of your creative endeavor, exploring new restaurants, and visiting your local horticultural center, bookstore, or farmers' market. Whatever makes you feel fired up embodies the essential element of inspiration! Here are some additional actions that can stoke your inspiration from real Bright Way practitioners:

- Think back to writing retreats and destination workshops I've attended. What thrilled me? What do I still remember fondly?
- Walk through a local museum.
- Find interesting artists who are improvising in their work.
- Be in nature; receive inspiration from nature's designs.
- Explore cultures from all parts of the world to spark more inspiration in myself.

FILTER THROUGH THE ESSENTIAL ELEMENT OF ARTISTRY (WATER) ▽

Ask yourself: *What artistic needs does my intention have?* Call on water to help your artistry flow, and use ▽. Lean on the Three Pillars of Artistry: beginner's mind, presence, and deep listening. How can you uphold these pillars in your creative life? Review the suggestions on pages 115–17. Here are some additional real-life artistry actions:

- Do a writing exercise in which I use no descriptive words to bring mood about, only dialogue, physical description, and setting.
- Think of what animal I most embody onstage. What do I want the audience to see when they look at me? Hear me?
- Cross-train: notice how musical my speaking voice is, and replicate my phrase shapes on the piano in terms of dynamics, tempo, and articulation.
- Record my improvisations and listen to them deeply, then ask others to listen and give me feedback as well.
- Focus on each individual tone, deeply listening to its color and character.

FILTER THROUGH THE ESSENTIAL ELEMENT OF LEARNING (AIR) △

Ask yourself: *What learning needs does my intention have?* Call on air to clear a spacious learning environment for you, and use △. You'll find out more about the essential element of learning in Bright Way step three; for now, consider how mental and intellectual energies support your creative endeavors. These include learning facts about your art, such as music theory or color theory, learning video programs that support your art (Scrivener, thank you!), and any other cerebral activities. Here are some additional real-life learning actions:

- Research roaming retreats. What are they doing right, according to attendee reviews?
- Watch two or three different performances of the character Stella in the play *A Streetcar Named Desire*, preferably from very different actors. What do I like about their performances? What can I incorporate into my process? Is there anything that feels inauthentic that I might want to avoid in my own expression?
- Take a class on the Dadaists.
- Listen to a piece to get it into my auditory memory, then analyze it via music theory, and then start working on the kinesthetic memory aspect (memorizing the choreography of the hands consciously versus by muscle memory alone).
- Study the rhythms of Middle Eastern and Indian music.

FILTER THROUGH THE ESSENTIAL ELEMENT OF TECHNIQUE (EARTH) ▽

Ask yourself: *What technique needs does my intention have?* Call on earth to ground your technique, and use ▽. Technique applies to anything that cultivates your practical skill in your creative endeavor and/or addresses your physical needs. You'll learn more about technique/earth in Bright Way step four; for now, jot down the first notions that come to mind. Here are some additional real-life technique actions:

- Practice my delivery of my open-mic piece, taking care to pause between words and sentences.
- Work on physicality. Try not to stay in one place for too long while delivering a line.
- Improve my use of cross-hatching and shading to create depth in my pencil drawings.
- Do vocal warm-ups before practicing.
- Optimize my sleep and nutrition, and keep going to exercise classes such as tai chi and Pilates.

FILTER THROUGH THE ESSENTIAL ELEMENT OF COMMUNITY (SPIRIT) O

Ask yourself: *What community needs does my intention have?* Call on spirit to connect you in grand community, and use O. Community at its core means connection, the ultimate aim of creativity. You'll encounter community/spirit more fully in Bright Way step five; for now, consider how spirit and community can enliven your creative path. How about starting up a harp circle? Joining a group of like-minded spiritual seekers? Volunteering somewhere? Here are some additional real-life community actions:

- Schedule a coffee meeting with a friend to ask about his experiences as a travel guide.
- Attend improv class more regularly. Get used to riffing off other actors.
- Attend gallery openings, and try to talk to one other artist at each one.
- Get feedback from friends, and find a group to play with.

- Continue to work on personal healing so that my highest spirit self flows through my music.

BRIGHT WAY ACTIVITY
Write Your Intentions

Just as you did with your purpose, write out your intentions and post them in places you often see: your desk, music stand, computer screen, phone screensaver; in your car, on the bathroom mirror, on the fridge. Your intentions are your true priorities. Keep them front and center!

Completing Step Two: Prioritize Your Intentions

You now have two or three purpose-driven intentions, plus a number of essential elemental actions for each intention. Well done! Reread your beautiful intentions. Fill yourself up with their magic. Engrave your intentions on your body, mind, and spirit like watermarks, gentle and constant reminders of what really matters to you.

> Your intentions are your true priorities. Keep them front and center!

Bask in all the work you've done here in Bright Way step two. It takes a lot of guts to buck the status quo and honestly listen to your heart. Some of the gains from your hard work will show up immediately, and some will manifest over a lifetime.

What I know for sure is that you are filling up with the replenishing energy of your true self, right this very moment. You inspire me! Your story is being told through your intentions, and as philosopher Martha Nussbaum says, "you can't really change the heart without telling a story." So, thank you for your openness and efforts. I'll see you in Bright Way step three: create your practicum plan, where we get down to the *how* of manifesting your purposeful intentions — *the how of making your story come true.*

Step Three: Create Your Practicum Plan

Prepare to Fly: Map Your Dreams

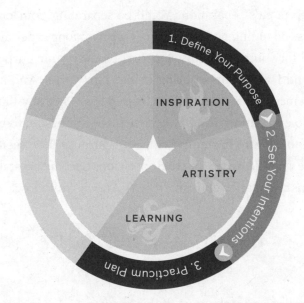

You are now familiar with the creative power of cycles and how switching modes gives you new energy and insight. We've been in an intuitive, receptive mode until now. Thank you for being willing to open yourself to our journey thus far. It takes courage to be this vulnerable, gentle, and loving toward yourself. We cycle on, switching to direct action and clear structure. It's time to draw up your practical action plan for your purpose and intentions so that they can take flight! It's time for Bright Way step three: create your practicum plan.

Keen Thinking and Rational Plans

Your practicum plan channels your magic into skill. Since this step is about rational plans and keen thinking, airy learning is your essential element ally. *Learning how to learn* gets your plans off the ground so that your intentions soar. And your natural element ally for this step, air, breezes in with clarity, decisiveness, and freshness.

Your alchemical operation now advances to *separation*. During separation, you make active decisions about what to keep and what to discard. The root meaning of separation is "to pull apart and make ready, to prepare." You experienced fiery initiation during calcination. Dissolution's honoring of emotional depth got you in touch with your deepest desires. These have both prepared you for analytical Bright Way step three's separation. You'll be separating your creative materials into clear tactics and timing and letting go of what no longer pertains.

I'm excited for you to take this step, first because your purpose is a thing of great beauty, and I want you to bring it into our world. And second, because I've seen the tremendous ripple effects this step has. They say that as you do one thing, so you do everything. By giving structure to your creative life, you invite your entire life to fall into harmony with your purpose. I've seen this phenomenon give people a new lease on life; their decisions become crystal clear, meaning that their actions also clarify and amplify. As Above, So Below!

BRIGHT WAY ACTIVITY
Invoke Air △

Turn to the diagram at the start of this chapter. Color in the step three / learning pie piece, using whatever color invokes air for you. Feel clarity blow through you as you do. If you have no color writing utensils, move on to part two of this activity: draw the alchemical symbol for air (△) inside the pie piece and even breezing down the page. Feel the flighty energy of the upward triangle being tempered by the line, reflecting the spaciousness of air being contained within the atmosphere of our Earth.

Where You Are Now

Now that we're in practical mode, let's recap what you've accomplished. Thus far, you have identified:

1. Your purpose
2. Your intentions, accompanied by essential elemental actions for your intentions

Bravo! This is much further than many creatives go. Even if you stopped right here, your journey would already be worth it. But why stop when there is so much joy and expansion yet to come? You're about to take on one of the most exciting jobs you'll ever have: being your best teacher.

Let's now set up the structure that will undergird you practicum plan. We start by reorienting our learning approach back to the Bright Way core principles of growth and joy.

Everyone Can Learn

We gain Bright Knowledge and inspiration from others; this is integral to the Bright Way. Past wisdom cannot be replaced. However, to fully absorb all this knowledge and inspiration, ultimately we must become our own teachers.

Each of us learns differently. And it is up to each of us to discover our personal learning style. I've taught and learned in almost every schooling environment I can imagine: public school, private school, alternative schools, religious schools, big universities, tiny colleges, European conservatories, home schooling environments, online classes, private lessons, huge workshops, and the list goes on. I've also taught pupils from ages two to ninety-two (so far), from Montessori group music classes where we danced and sang and I broke up wrestling matches between piles of toddler boys, to the spritely senior who took up piano after a seventy-five-year hiatus. Here's what I learned from all these experiences: no one curriculum fits all, and every person learns differently.

Further, I'm convinced that everyone can learn. A few encounters that taught me this beyond a shadow of a doubt spring to mind.

> Ultimately we must become our own teachers.

One day a mother called up requesting harp lessons for her young daughter, with the caveat that her girl had been diagnosed with several learning disabilities that would probably hinder her progress in music. A few days later, in walked a lively and serious little girl. We got right to harping. She addressed the strings without hesitation, reveling in the different sound colors she brought out. It wasn't long before she was composing her own twenty-minute songs, complete with narration, musical interludes, and special effects. She even corralled her proud mother — a dedicated amateur musician herself — into a recital performance, incorporating the family's impressive and unusual instrument collection with ease. This from a girl who had been deemed unlikely to achieve much musically! I was struck by this girl's ability to work with the big picture. She built long narrative arcs that kept her audiences spellbound. Her interdisciplinary management was impressive. I didn't bother her much with note reading or theory — even though these are key ways that I learn personally — because these arenas only frustrated her. Instead, *I capitalized on her unique strengths*. Her loving parents used the same approach, and it paid off. Now a young woman, she currently holds a PhD from a prestigious university and works as a young professor abroad. Quite a contrast to what had been predicted for her!

> No one curriculum fits all, and every person learns differently.

Another anecdote concerns a boy who was also diagnosed with various learning disabilities. His case was more severe, to the point where graduating from high school was in question. As we worked together at the piano, a passionate and inquiring soul emerged. When we focused on what he was interested in, there was no end to how deeply he would dig, but if I tried to get him to do anything he wasn't passionate about, he balled up in a rage. Thankfully, in private lessons I have the leeway to do whatever I feel is best instead of having to follow a particular agenda or curriculum. As we worked together, his love of singing came to the fore, so much so that I recommended he focus completely on it. Next thing you know, he was singing solos in semi-professional musicals, adoring the spotlight, becoming interested in acting, a picture of confidence. Where once it seemed he might not graduate from high school, today he's a high school teacher, and as a sweet sidenote, I played harp at his wedding a few years ago. Life is beautiful! If you've ever felt a lack of confidence in your learning ability, think back on these stories.

Very few people get the opportunity to access their perfect learning environment. People find themselves attached to systems, methods, and labels that hamper their learning or at least slow them down considerably. This is structure gone wrong. Let's build a healthy structure that staunchly supports *you.*

Know this: *you were born to learn.* It's our human nature. We're wired for learning from day one. And the more research that comes out, the more it's proven that learning is a lifelong ability. Take heart: when you identify your personal learning style, you can learn at any age, time, and place.

> When you identify your personal learning style, you can learn at any age, time, and place.

I've seen musicians finally learn to memorize music after decades of believing they couldn't; to improvise even though they thought that was only for experts; to record and deal with technology decades younger than themselves. I know you can master the skills of your creative field, too. Taking our cue from Aristotle, let's *understand* your learning style so that you become your best teacher:

Those who know, do. Those that understand, teach.

— ARISTOTLE, paraphrased by Lee Shulman

BRIGHT WAY BREAK
Get Some Air

Stale or warm air often makes us complacent and sleepy. Similarly, we can't grow as creatives when our teaching methods or knowledge have stagnated. Open the windows. Turn on your ceiling fan. Create a cross-breeze by propping open your doors. Go outside for some fresh air. As you do, meditate on the air flowing over and around you. Is it cool or warm? Does it hold the scent memory of another time or place? Does it bring the promise of rain and renewal? How can these sensory reflections help to make room for newer, kinder, more exciting learning practices?

Take a Stand for Your Imperfect Creative Self

When it comes to taking creative action, there are so many options that we can easily get overwhelmed. Further, our lives are full, and trying to fit our creativity in can feel daunting. As we move into practical mode in this step, keep in mind that perfection in any arena is not our Bright Way. Rather, we aim for engaged, creative, free yet connected lives, and these look more like rainforests than manicured lawns. Let's meet some creatives with busy-yet-fulfilled lives, starting with mother and musician Monica Schley:

"With a baby, I always feel like there's a ticking timer at nap time. I try to squeeze in moments to write or practice, but I never know how long it will be. I create lists of how to prioritize: #1 practice music for gig tonight; #2 transcribe a piece if I have time; #3 blast out my recording to one agency. If I can do that much, *awesome*! Sometimes only one thing gets accomplished, and if someone has a fever or a field trip, forget about it. I have to be real about the current daily situation of food, laundry, school lunch, diapers, etc.!

"When I had my first kiddo, I blended my writing and music together sort of by accident. Once I stopped gigging late-night shows, I began songwriting. The poetry morphed into lyrics instead. I had to become selective about what I said yes to. Would I take a club gig at 10 PM? No way, not unless it paid well (insert laugh). Eventually, people stopped asking me, but that's okay. Because I changed.

"I won't lie. Sometimes I find myself lamenting over the artists who have more freedom. It takes so much time to polish a craft, and I never feel like I have enough anymore. I don't have a stuckness; I have a restriction. This is interesting, though, because motherhood is also the blessing that allowed me to open up into a new form! I started singing in public. I wrote enough songs to record an album. I formed a band (The Daphnes), and now I can be the leader and call the shots to what fits my lifestyle. I probably wouldn't have been organized enough to do this without motherhood 'restricting' me, and half my songs are inspired in some way by the process of being mom. So it's a two-sided coin. A yin-yang.

"Being a musician mama has made me just practice with a toddler in my lap and accept that I might be winging it at the gig a little more. It's maddening! It's terrifying! It's exciting! It's liberating!"

Mothers like Monica are at the vanguard of exposing the toxicity of our disconnected world. Their stories reflect the bind creatives often feel suffocated by. Like many other people, mothers frequently juggle multiple jobs and roles that are undervalued. Why should they try to fit perfectly into an imperfect system? *For that matter, why should any of us?* Full-time pediatric intensive care nurse and mother of four (and beloved sister of your author!) Sophie Kelliher also rejects conforming to the status quo:

"You have to create the time for yourself to be creative and not look at it as selfish. If some of the housework or gardening or making fancy dinners goes to the side, then that's the way it is. No one will give you a medal for doing any of these things anyway, and you'll suffer if you don't make time for yourself.

"I've been spending time every day working out, and I just make it work. Kids are happy if you are happy. I just have to be a bit more organized. Online food shopping, and no excuses.

"Make your hour a priority. It's only an hour. For whatever it is you want to do, commit and find the discipline to tune out other thoughts or duties and create some self-love.

"You deserve the time to yourself. Mom guilt is real when you work full-time. But when it's just an hour, and you'll feel like yourself again and not just like the parent or the wife or whatever, it's worth it. The oven won't clean itself, but I don't give a ****. You only have one life to live. Any restrictions are usually self-inflicted. Break the wheel."

> Whatever your circumstances, you can live an engaged and creative life. Starting now.

We can learn a lot from these two mothers and their ability to practice the keen discernment of alchemical separation to such a degree. For skill, they employ tactical measures such as scheduling, streamlining chores, and being realistic about how pristine their houses need to be. They also honor their magic by taking a firm stand for what they enjoy doing. They recognize their heart's desire and value their creativity as things of inherent worth. Their bright, aligned energy radiates out, inspiring us all — do you feel it? They show us that whatever your circumstances, you can live an engaged and creative life. Starting now.

Expand Your Energy

When it comes down to actually practicing — whatever that means for your creative endeavor — finding enough energy in the midst of busy lives is something many of us struggle with. So that you will be set up optimally before you even start practicing, I offer you these three techniques for aerating and refreshing your energy.

Uncover Time/Space Pockets

- Repurpose material and projects, as Monica did by converting her poetry into songwriting (and our email conversation into a blog post)!
- Combine compatible activities, such as working on your art while your children do homework, listening to books as you drive, writing while on public transportation, or reviewing course material while you're standing in line.

- Recognize that child-rearing, day jobs, and anything you are actively engaged in can be creative acts. What creative grist for the mill can you glean from your experiences? How can you be even more creatively involved in your work? How can you use these opportunities to cultivate Sacred Reciprocity? Raising children, for instance, teaches us about human nature, desires, and learning styles, and it can even unlock insights into our own childhoods. Honor what you do as creativity in action.

- Leverage cross-training. As you write that work email, notice your writing style, your communication style. Make your emails even more expressive and aligned with Sacred Reciprocity. Use dishwashing or weeding time to practice singing, breathing, memorizing a poem, or reciting back the steps you're learning here on our Bright Way!

- Outsource and automate whatever you can, such as having groceries delivered and bills paid automatically. Eliminating tasks greatly alleviates decision fatigue!

- Say no. Go back and count how many times Sophie and Monica said no to people and things. If they didn't, there would clearly be zero time left for them and their creativity. Consider how this may be the case for you right now.

> Honor what you do as creativity in action.

> Anything you are actively engaged in can be a creative act.

Tap Into Your Core Connection

You've experienced that when you harmonize with yourself (see page 97), you access your true power, sheer life force. Harmonize with yourself regularly to top off your energy battery. The beginning of each creative session, when you're standing in line at the grocery store, when you're waiting for a client to show up: these are all excellent opportunities to harmonize. Over time, you'll most likely find yourself feeling generally brighter and stronger. Try it and see.

And you have another set of beautiful energizers that represent your core connection: your purpose and your intentions. Recall these, and fill up with joy. Joy energizes!

Minimize Mental Drains

Negative self-talk is a huge energy drain, which is why we've already learned multiple techniques for sidestepping it. A major source of negative talk — self- and otherwise — is social media, which in my experience is one of the biggest energy drains of all. Taking my own advice about avoiding negativity, allow me to simply suggest that you experiment with a social media and news diet for three days. Temporarily restrict your access to social media sites, or set them to power down after a few minutes. Notice what effects this has on you.

Note: your social media diet doesn't have to include direct communication with people you care about or access to learning resources. Nonetheless, see if you can convert these connections into more engaged encounters. Try video-conferencing rather than just texting; print out those transcripts and hold them in your hands rather than only watching the video. How do these actions affect your energy levels?

Another big mental energy drain is fretting over scheduling. Trying to remember when and where everything is leads to brain overload. This is yet another reason that we create a practicum plan in Bright Way step three! Before we do that, let's carry on circulating our energy with another Bright Way Break.

BRIGHT WAY BREAK
Freedom Through Breathing

Air being our elemental ally for this step, we focus on our breathing again, which is such a source of inspiration (literally!) and energy. Pause, breathe several breaths, and say to yourself, "I am here. I am held. I am whole." Notice how you feel during and after your break. Do you sense more clarity? Do you feel more spaciousness?

Create Your Practicum Plan

Tapping into the power of cycles, your practicum plan comprises two coexisting cycles:

- **Mastery Actions to Performance Actions.** This is the cycle from learning to performing/sharing. In this cycle, you set up your plan for how to learn, leading to mastery. From there, your plan for how to practice for performance/sharing becomes apparent. And upon performing/sharing your work, you'll often get ideas for further refinement, cycling you back to the mastery stage.

- **Long-Term to Daily Plans.** This cycle starts with your long-term intentions and makes a plan for how you will manifest them. The cycle then telescopes down to the daily actions needed to support your long-term intentions. As you live creatively day to day, you get immediate feedback on how important your long-term intentions are, and the cycle continues.

Using both these cycles, setting priorities becomes straightforward, always relevant, and meaningful.

Figure 9. Mastery to Performance Action + Planning Cycles

Though different in focus, these cycles support each other. Understanding the connections and contrasts *between and within each cycle itself* makes all the difference between creating with confidence and giving up in frustration.

For example, how we practice in order to master skills often requires the opposite approach to how we practice for performance. Acting on this fact alone can radically improve both your learning results and your performance confidence. We'll dive much deeper into this as we walk the Bright Way steps. As a brief preview, mastery is all about *precision*: focusing on small chunks, repeating, stopping and starting, going over the thing with a fine-toothed comb. Performance, on the other hand, is all about *flow*: sharing your piece in one fell swoop as an entity in itself. Because precision and flow are polar opposites — related, yet different in degree — it's important to have distinct practice plans for each stage.

> How we practice in order to master skills often requires the opposite approach to how we practice for performance.

Similarly, making a distinction between long-term and daily plans keeps you from getting stuck in the day-to-day weeds. And, conversely, it keeps you from ambling through your creative life without a bigger picture to guide you. Further, long-term and daily plans support each other. Fueled by your long-term plans, you appreciate how each of your small daily actions propels you forward. In turn, living your daily plans throws light on how relevant your intentions are, alerting you to change, if needed.

BRIGHT WAY ACTIVITY
Take Your Temperature

Do you practice differently when you're first learning something versus when you're about to share or complete it?

For example, when you're first starting out, are you focused on small details, working word by word, stitch by stitch? And then when you're getting ready to share it, are you feeling more of the overall arc of your story, the drape of your entire creation rather than the microscopic details? Or do you dive in and let the thing come together bit by bit more intuitively, and then drill down during the polishing stage?

Jot down your impressions. This is a quick temperature read on where you are structure-wise. You'll be learning a lot more about how to build these structures soon.

> # BRIGHT WAY BREAK
> ## *Let Yourself Be Breathed*

Sit quietly and allow yourself to breathe in and out gently. Close your eyes. Sense how your breath happens effortlessly, as if your breath is breathing you. How does this ease feel? Imagine bringing this ease to your learning and practice. Now allow your mind to clear, and simply enjoy this moment of freedom.

Mastery Check-In

We start building your practicum plan by gathering your primary materials: your intentions and how you plan to act on them. Take these mastery check-in actions now:

1. **Take out your Bright Way Diary.** Look at your purpose and the two or three intentions you created in Bright Way step two. Reconnect to them and get completely fired up by them.

2. **Turn to a page halfway through your Bright Way Diary, and rewrite your intentions.** Give each intention its own page for ample space — you'll need it!

    Tip: You've been keeping your practicum plan in the same diary as your purpose and intentions so that you can notice how interconnected everything is. Some colorful sticky notes or dividers can help you track the sections of your diary. As you get more familiar with the Bright Way System, you may prefer to have a master Bright Way Diary for big-picture work and a dedicated practicum journal for daily logging. Or keep everything in one place! You'll know what is right for you.

3. **Refer back to your essential element actions for your intentions.** For each of your intentions, pick out the single most appealing action for each essential element. We're motivated by emotion and the anticipation of rewarding actions (dopamine rises exponentially with the anticipation of things going well — even more than when they actually do!). So fuel your practicum plan with compelling actions. Write your chosen actions on their intention pages, drawing the relevant alchemical symbols beside them.

    So, for your first intention, you'll have:

    - one inspiration action △
    - one artistry action ▽
    - one learning action ⩟
    - one technique action ⩛
    - one community action O

      ...for a total of five actions for each intention.

4. **Repeat this process for your remaining intentions.**

Long-Term Planning

I like to joke that scheduling is the hardest art of all. I've seen many creatives (myself included) sit down to plan their schedule, only to gasp at the realization that they have no time left for learning and creativity. Mapping out your creative time is diagnostic, revealing a hidden problem in our creative lives: we have set aside no time for creativity!

The back-and-forth dance of "should I / shouldn't I practice?" is exhausting. Schedule your creative time so that you don't have to think twice and can jump straight into your work without debate. Take a stand for creativity in your schedule. Defend your purpose by giving it pride of place in your schedule!

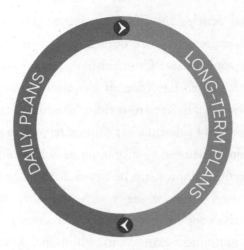

Figure 10. The Long-Term to Daily Planning Cycle

As with anything else, scheduling is a skill you can build. No one is born a talented scheduler. It's never too late to learn how to do it. I'm still learning and am far from perfect. But I'd be way worse off if I didn't try! Use these long-term scheduling guidelines, modifying them to suit your circumstances:

> *Defend your purpose by giving it pride of place in your schedule!*

1. Review your calendar for the next two weeks.
2. Prioritizing your best energy times, schedule your creativity dates based on the following questions:

When do I have the most energy? All of us have particular bodily rhythms. These are the times when we're high or low in energy. Are you a morning person? If so, try to engage with your creativity then. I know it's tempting to respond to the clamors of the beginning of the day. But then you're spending your best energy on those things rather than on your creativity. When that "free time" finally rolls around, you're too tired to engage. Learning and creativity both suffer.

If you're a night owl like me, trying to force yourself to be creative early in the day is an exercise in comedy. Sometimes I wonder what happened to my brain overnight. It just isn't able to get into gear as early as other people's. When I honor this truth and work later in the day, everything comes out far better.

I know that countless articles and lifestyle coaches claim you should get up at 5:00 AM and have your creative work done before your household awakes. If I tried that, this book would be, well, nonexistent.

Fun note: once you start fueling yourself adequately, you may find that your best energy times change or expand. Keep responding to yourself as creativity in action!

How much time shall I schedule? It's ultimately up to you to discover what suits you. Keep in mind that even twenty minutes of focused time can garner big results. And that twenty minutes can be divided into two ten-minute sessions. The key is to be focused during whatever time you have. Twenty focused minutes are worth more than one hour of distracted practice.

How long is your attention span? Work within that. Over time, by following the Bright Way, you'll most likely find that your attention span increases. Notice how long you can focus *before* you start feeling tired. Because once you're tired, practicing through physical and/or mental fog can actually impede your learning and creativity. Respect your energy.

How many days a week shall I schedule? Research suggests that taking one day off actually helps with the learning process. Your brain gets a chance to digest everything you've learned. Beyond that, it's a personal decision how many days a week are best. I recommend aiming for five days a week to start. If that feels like too much, four is fine. Lower than that, and you may not gain enough momentum to feel satisfied with your progress. It's important to feel good about what you do, as this is a major driver of inspiration (which will take care of most of your motivation!).

> *Short, sweet, and **often** are the bywords.*

Skill building is like physical activity. Small, regular chunks of activity are better than one long marathon a week. As with exercise, if you go for one blowout session a week, you'll end up frustrated and possibly injured. *Short, sweet*, and *often* are the bywords here. There are, of course, outliers. I remember one harpist who practiced six weeks in a row because she felt so enthusiastic. When she asked me if this was okay, I had to say yes. Joy leads! Experiment, and be your best teacher.

How do I schedule for deadlines? What if you've got a show, lesson, or submission deadline coming up? First, plan on being ready before your due date. This gives you space to refine, plus wiggle room, should any unforeseen circumstances come up (the latter being close to 100 percent likely, in my experience). Then work backward. Break down what needs to be completed by your deadline into specific milestones. Schedule in your milestones, moving backward in your calendar from your (early!) due date.

A Word on Deadlines and Due Dates

Deadlines / due dates can be allies or enemies on the creative path. I've found in my own personal creative work that deadlines (I'll use *deadline* from now on for brevity's sake and because I like the extra nudge that word gives me — always go with what fits you best!) are crucial for me. I love researching, learning, and experimenting. Because of that, I can stay indefinitely in exploration mode, meaning I wouldn't actually complete anything and share it with the world.

Having deadlines keeps me organized. With a deadline, I can set priorities and get things finished (although as we know, nothing is ever perfect, and here I am, making additions and tweaks a day before my final deadline for this book).

The key to keeping deadlines my ally rather than my enemy is to remember why I'm doing the thing. For example, I've had many deadlines for this book as it progressed through its various stages of gestation. Remembering every single time *why* I'm writing this book, and that the deadlines are helping me, means I feel supported rather than oppressed. And my "why" for writing this book? It's my purpose: to return to my true self and thereby encourage others to do the same. A purpose that makes me thank deadlines for making me actually get this message out!

BRIGHT WAY ACTIVITY
Deadlines as Allies

Consider your relationship with deadlines. Are you friends? Acquaintances? Not on speaking terms? Write your reflections in your Bright Way Diary. Then reflect again and see how/if deadlines can become more like allies rather than enemies to you. You may find that deadlines are not relevant to your creative path, which is fine. The important thing is to discover what is most helpful for you and your creative journey.

BRIGHT WAY BREAK
Sit Quietly

You may find that by taking frequent breaks, you can work longer and/or more deeply. Paradoxically, by stopping you go further in the long run. Neuropsychologist and musician Teresa Bailey shares this story:

> Hikers in Switzerland tend not to go blazing up the hill the way some American hikers do. They walk slowly and steadily, and take frequent breaks to admire where they are. By doing this they often cover more ground than hikers who start out strong but deplete their energy more quickly. A Swiss couple I knew were astounded at how hikers were approaching the hike up Half Dome in Yosemite at the beginning of the trail. This couple were some of the slowest walkers at the start, but their round-trip time was significantly shorter and more pleasant as they passed others looking exhausted and pained from pushing too hard too fast.

Take a moment to let these words from the medieval mystic St. Catherine of Siena flow through you:

> *Daily struggles we know.*
> *Sit quiet for a minute, dear.*
> *Feel the wind,*
> *Let the light touch you.*

Daily Planning Guidelines

Having covered mastery and long-term planning, let's now telescope down to daily planning, your day-to-day practice plan. In your Bright Way Diary, turn to a new page, maybe a few pages beyond your last intention entry.

Start with a small number of intentions per day. Even just one or two is great! Pick one to three essential element actions per intention. Rewrite these actions into your daily plan. By rewriting your intentions and actions, you embed them deeper into your memory, setting you up for solid learning and imaginative creativity. As an example, this could look like:

Intention: memorize two more measures of "Skye Boat Song"
Actions: (1) Listen to my chosen two measures being played by my teacher on my slow-down app; (2) put these measures on repeat and sing along until I can sing them on my own; (3) play these measures on the harp (with or without printed music in front of me), one measure at a time.

Now let's look at your daily practice plan template:

1. Write down the date and your daily practice intentions and actions. Ask yourself:

   • What am I going to practice / work on today? This encompasses which intentions and actions you'll focus on.
   • What results am I aiming for today? This encompasses practical progress details, such as "I want to have memorized the first two measures of 'Skye Boat Song'" or "I intend to finish another page of writing."

2. End each practice session on a positive note, no matter how badly things went! This creates a positive association with practice rather than a demoralized one. Feeling positive about practice makes all the difference between coming back for more and giving up in defeat. Examples of ending on a positive note is recalling past successes such as rereading a poem you're particularly proud of, taking out your sketchbook and letting yourself just doodle, or playing/singing one beautiful note on your instrument.

3. Immediately after practice, log what you did and what results you got. Self-reflection and self-assessment accelerate your learning

significantly. Do this right after practice, because within seconds we start forgetting what we discovered. Capture these precious findings immediately. Building on our "Skye Boat Song" example above, you might write something like: "I found I could sing along with the recording of the piece but felt insecure when I went to the harp with it. When I sang along as I played the melody, I noticed I relaxed and made fewer mistakes because my hands seemed to follow wherever my voice led me."

4. **Based on what you discovered in your practice session, plan your follow-up actions for your next session.** This creates an enticing starting point for your next practice. You'll just glance at your notes and then be off and running! You might enjoy ending on a cliff-hanger, such as "I only went through half of X today, so I want to complete it next time." This satisfies our human urge to finish a story, and gives you a place to pick up immediately at the start of your next practice session.

And there we have it, your daily plan!

Your Step Three Essential Element: Learning (Air) △

We've ignited through the fire of the essential element of inspiration in step one (△). We've flowed with the water of the essential element of artistry in step two (▽). Now let's take to the air via the essential element of learning in step three (△).

Air represents clearing space, breezing in with new ideas, change, and clarity. Keep these associations, and any others you have with air, in mind when you're teaching yourself and learning. Call in the element of air, breathing freshness into your creative journey. Feel its cleansing breeze waft over you, reinvigorating you. Let its clarity help you see things in a new light. Learning often has heavy, stifling associations from our past. These might include unpleasant school experiences or stress from trying to master something under a brutal deadline. Let air blow away any old cobwebs.

Learning how to learn is a major part of being your best teacher. Welcome the essential element of learning onto your journey, knowing it is here to help, not judge you. Consider what learning means to you right now, in truthful clarity. Are old ghosts haunting you with scary stories about your learning capacities? Now is the time to expose them to air and let them float away. Two thousand years ago, Plato already understood this: "Knowledge which is acquired under compulsion obtains no hold on the mind...lessons that enter the soul against its will never grow roots and will never be preserved inside it." You're about to liberate your learning!

How to Be Your Own Best Teacher

We all face some common realities regarding learning. Honor these four learning realities, and your retention of new concepts — and your creative ability to use them — will soar.

Short and Sweet!

LEARNING REALITY ONE: SMALL IS BEAUTIFUL

I'll start with the learning reality that meets with the most resistance, both from my students and myself. Incredibly, given the amount of information coming at us every day, research shows that we can hold only between five and nine pieces of information in our short-term memory. Short-term memory is where new ideas and information is first stored in our minds. And how long does short-term memory last? A mere fifteen to thirty seconds.

Are these figures different from what you might have guessed? They took me aback when I first heard them! There will always be folks who are able to retain either more or less information, but five to nine pieces of information lasting fifteen to thirty seconds is a reasonable place to start. Let's use this information to our advantage.

Our learning aim is retention, the ability to recall information and act on it. This fosters mastery. Put another way, our learning goal is to transform short-term memory items into long-term memory access.

Our first order of business is to bite off a chunk of information small enough to chew on. This is what is meant by "work in small chunks," which you've probably heard many times before. Trying to cram in more information than your five to nine pieces is exactly like trying to download more data when the hard drive is running out of space. The whole system freezes and might even crash.

Here's where many people get stuck: How small are these chunks, exactly? To answer, think about what a piece of information is for you personally. This can be confusing, and no wonder: the definition of a "piece of information" is different for everyone! Luckily, there's a quick way to determine what your personal piece is. It is whatever you can perceive in one go. Your piece is a pattern that you understand as one item. It might be tiny or huge, depending on your skill level. This pattern is something you can understand and recall immediately. Let's now clarify what patterns actually are.

> Our learning goal is to transform short-term memory items into long-term memory access.

Perceive Patterns

LEARNING REALITY TWO:
PATTERN RECOGNITION IS THE FOUNDATION OF MEMORY

As we gain mastery in a field, we perceive and can *actively work with* increasingly complex patterns. Think back to when you first started reading: it was all you could do to recognize the letter *A*. In fact, *A* itself had to be broken down into three lines: a tent with a bar crossing it (rather like our air symbol △!). These days the pattern *A* is so ingrained in your long-term memory that you breezed right past the more than thirty *A*s in this very paragraph! Not to mention that they were mostly lowercase, and you still recognized them.

In the same way, by repeating our little chunks we start to collate them into patterns. This happens in all arenas of creativity (and life). For example, in the beginning, musicians have to think hard about individual notes. We may take weeks learning ABCDEFG. They look like seven different items at first. Over time, though, we collate these individual notes into higher-level patterns such as chords. For example, C-E-G makes a C chord. That's three items (C-E-G) now whittled down to one item (C chord). Later, we recognize chord combinations such as V-I (dominant-tonic is another way to name this pattern) as the triumphant ending of many songs. Eventually we recognize entire forms such as the twelve-bar blues as one chunk.

Does this sound overwhelming? It is if you bite off too much at once. "Move from the known to the unknown, and make it known," as we heard earlier. If you don't group information into patterns, you'll jump from the known to the unknown *to the even greater unknown*. Before you know it, you'll be lost.

What may seem overwhelming to a beginner might look simple to a more advanced practitioner. This is not because the more experienced person is smarter or more talented (perish the word). It's simply that they have more complex pattern recognition. They can bite off seemingly bigger chunks, and chew them. How? It might have looked like magic, but now you know the trick.

Imagine trying to memorize a page-long poem by reading it top to bottom over and over. Then picture learning it line by line, or in even smaller chunks. Which approach will help you master the entire poem more effectively? Without a doubt, when you memorize it in smaller chunks you will be more successful. If you take the more devil-may-care attitude, there's a great chance you will never memorize the poem at all, no matter how many times you try. The problem? Simply that you chose too large a chunk.

I see creatives of all sorts being choked by biting off too much. I still do it myself sometimes. Many people doubt their intelligence and even their sanity when practice doesn't bring progress. Yet of course they're as clever and creative as ever! The problem is that they've overloaded their hard drive, as it were, or have their mouths so full they can't chew.

Creativity involves engaging with material in such a way that you put your stamp on it. It's not enough simply to mimic discrete patterns. To create something of meaning, you need to string patterns together so that they make sense as a whole. Your work gains integrity when you bring elements together in such a way that they shed new light on each other. Patterns are creativity's foundation and worthy of diligent cultivation.

There are no shortcuts. Imagine having never integrated five letters from the alphabet. What would reading be like for you, no matter how basic the book? Instead, here you are flying through these sentences, barely noticing the complex activity you've mastered because you have repeated — practiced — it so much. If you have small, fundamental gaps in your skills, the results can be the same as our five-letters-short reader. A tiny blank in your knowledge — even something as tiny as not knowing *A* — can stall your creative process. Why? Because blanks break pattern formation. You can't perceive patterns when there are missing pieces. This might sound alarming, but the fix is simple, as our four learning realities demonstrate.

> Patterns are creativity's foundation and worthy of diligent cultivation.

Honor Your Learning Style

Learning Reality Three: We Each Have a Personal Learning Style

Research on learning grows by leaps and bounds every year. We keep discovering new ways that people learn. It's always good news. For example, we've discovered that, contrary to common belief, we can grow neural pathways at any age. And so many other hopeful reports are coming out all the time.

It was a huge relief to many when the three major learning styles, auditory, visual, and kinesthetic, were identified. Much classroom learning is based only on auditory learning, such as lectures. Visual learning is addressed on occasion by presentations and demonstrations. Kinesthetic learning, however — direct experience, tactile engagement — rarely gets incorporated outside of dance and sports. With this in mind, if your favored learning style is visual or kinesthetic, then you would be at a disadvantage in many learning settings.

To remedy this, start to reclaim *your* learning style as your own teacher. This being a major focus on our Bright Way, you have done and will continue doing many activities to uncover your learning style. I believe there are more than just the three learning styles, auditory, visual, and kinesthetic. But for now, they're a solid place to start.

Consider: Are you more of a visual learner? If so, finding visual representations of your creative endeavor will be helpful. For example, if you're a gardener and want to learn about a certain potting technique, look for an illustrated how-to guide, or better yet, look for an online video tutorial. The power of modeling is striking. I remember a student coming to me for a lesson shortly after watching me in concert, and suddenly her technique had clicked into place. She said that observing me in flow for a solid hour-and-a-half caused everything that we had been working on to coalesce.

If you're a kinesthetic learner, go to someone who will show you the technique hands-on, or watch and work alongside a master gardener. As Teresa notes: "Kinesthetic learners often jump right in and start doing things they observe or that feel 'right,' and find ways to talk about it later, if at all."

And for the auditory learner, listening to talks, recordings of music, and other aural sources is the ticket.

Most of us employ a combination of these learning types. Determine your learning recipe, knowing that it also morphs over times and circumstances, as is the creative way. Maybe right now kinesthetic is your strongest style, auditory your second strongest, and visual your third strongest. Whatever your style, own it proudly and (re)arrange your learning practices to match it.

Making Friends With Mistakes!

LEARNING REALITY FOUR: MISTAKES ARE CRUCIAL ALLIES

If you're not making mistakes, you're doing it wrong. I'm sort of kidding, since *wrong* isn't a word I favor. Yet if we're not making mistakes, we aren't learning; we're simply retreading known ground. Mistakes give us feedback on what and how to improve. Mistakes can be lucky accidents in which we gain even better ideas and insight. Mistakes give us benchmarks for what we don't want to feel or do. Mistakes provide opportunities to reach out for help, fostering community and deeper learning for all. There's even evidence that mistakes make our brains grow. For sure I'm the kind of person who wears down the eraser long before the pencil is even a quarter done.

> If you're not making mistakes, you're not learning.

We'll be delving further into the benefits of mistakes, drafts, and other "portals of discovery," as James Joyce calls them, in Bright Way step four. In the meantime, mull over how you might reframe mistakes as essential assistants — allies! — rather than as enemies on your creative journey.

Review: The Four Learning Realities

1. Honor the fact that your brain holds approximately *five to nine separate pieces of information* for fifteen to thirty seconds in short-term memory. For you, a piece of information is *any pattern you can perceive in one go.*

2. By *stringing together known patterns and repeating them*, you integrate increasingly complex patterns. This is the key to achieving mastery and opening the door to creativity.

3. Identify your personal learning style(s) and (re)arrange your learning in alignment.

4. Make mistakes, and learn from them joyfully!

If you follow these four points alone, you will notice a huge improvement in your learning and therefore your creativity. And when we see results from our efforts, we are motivated to do even more. This is you being your best teacher!

BRIGHT WAY ACTIVITY
Your Learning Reality

Write the four learning realities into your Bright Way Diary. Which of the four is the most eye-opening to you? Why? Can you visualize how you might apply these learning approaches to your creative practice? Focus on a different learning reality for each of your next four practice sessions. After each of these practice sessions, log the insights and improvements you gained from each in your diary.

✦ ✦ ✦

From Mastery to Performance

As a musician, I'm used to practicing for mastery, which I define as practicing to gain the skill required to play a piece fluently. Keep in mind that we usually have different mastery standards for different scenarios. For example, you may aim for a very high level of mastery for a high-stakes situation, whereas for a more casual situation, you might be satisfied with less rigorous preparation.

Figure 11. The Mastery to Performance Actions Cycle

I didn't have the best mastery approaches back in the day because I didn't know the four learning realities. Nonetheless, my aim was to be able to play the piece well enough during a practice session at home or in the studio, which I could usually scrape through. Had I known of the learning realities, though, my mastery would have been much more solid.

However, when it came to performing, everything fell apart. Was I facing an instrument I'd never seen before? What on earth was going on? It took a long time to realize — in great part thanks to preparing my students for recitals — that while I had practiced for mastery, albeit haphazardly, *I had not practiced at all for performance*. Is there a difference? Yes, a dramatic one.

When we practice for mastery, we aim for precision. Precision takes the microview of working in small chunks, repeating them, and examining patterns. What a disastrous approach for performance! Can you imagine giving a performance in which you stop and start constantly and repeat sections over and over? Oh, wait, that's what was happening to me back in the day! The lightbulb went on.

Performance requires us to flow through the thing, come what may. A performance recites an entire experience. It paints a whole picture. Performance is not fragments; it is a complete entity.

And just like mastery, performance comes in many shades. You may want to perform for yourself alone, for life source, at works-in-progress gatherings, in hospitals or concert halls. The spectrum of practice for performance is wide, and likewise the degree of preparation required can be very different between scenarios. As with everything on our journey together, your direct experience will guide you to what is right for you.

Fundamentally, keep in mind this polarity: mastery is precision, while performance is flow. Honor them as individual entities that are different yet complementary, and as with their correspondences skill and magic, manifestation blooms.

But can you really practice for performance? Can the sensation of performing be replicated when you're not in front of an audience? Surprisingly, it can.

> Mastery is precision, while performance is flow.

Practicing Flow

Practicing flow looks a lot like our dream practice scenario: you get to fly from top to bottom in your work, with no breaks. If mistakes pop up, you're blessedly allowed to overlook them. You're going for the entire picture here. You're painting in broad strokes.

Trust that you've done your detailed work during mastery practice. You'll know you've mastered the matter in hand when it feels like a complete entity. For example, you have mastered a song when you can play it through with feeling and confidence. You have mastered a poem when you feel that click of recognition that no additions are necessary. You have mastered a dish when you sigh at its deliciousness.

Now it's time to share, that is perform, your creation. Let it rip! In Bright Way step four I'll give you specific recommendations for performance practice and cultivating flow. Writer, editor, and bassoonist Georgia Hughes gives us a preview of what performance practice entails for her: "One of the best pieces of advice I received from my teacher when preparing for a recital was when she told me to play through the full recital every day for the two weeks prior, no stopping. Wow. What an education in how many times I wanted to stop, and it really did teach me about stamina, breathing, pacing, and moving ahead."

Making the distinction between practicing for mastery and practicing for performance is key, so for each of your creative endeavors, note whether it's at the mastery or performance stage. This might be easier for creatives such as musicians, dancers, and actors. For others, such as visual artists and writers, for instance, mastery includes technical aspects such as literary devices and narrative structure, while performance includes more outward-facing, crowd-pleasing elements, such as making sure your short story has a catchy hook. Separating your practice into mastery and performance stages determines your practice approach and alerts you to when it's time to shift modes. We'll integrate all this in Bright Way step four.

When Mastery and Performance Practice Meet

Look back at the Mastery => Performance actions diagram on page 155. Notice that there is some overlap between mastery and practice. While I know it's key to make a distinction between what mastery practice looks like versus performance practice, the fact is, there is healthy overlap. Emma, our composer and producer whom you met back in "The Bright Way Ignites," shares her experience of synergizing mastery and performance approaches:

> "I was only ever taught 'mastery' techniques, and in some ways, that type of practice felt like a practice of looking for mistakes. The focus was always on what I was doing 'wrong' and what still had to be improved.
>
> "What I would have loved was to have been encouraged to practice 'flow'— even if it was only for myself! We don't have to wait to perform to allow ourselves to experience flow. Flow is the state of taking *pleasure* in our practice, finding joy in life. Giving yourself permission to not just focus on what needs to be continually improved but to release yourself to the pleasure of playing!

"So many of us wait until performance time to try to go into that state of pleasure and ecstasy. I'm wanting to experience that in my practice sessions now, even if just for five minutes, and even if it's just for myself. Because the first person who deserves to enjoy your art…is *you*."

Talk about being your best teacher! As with everything on our Bright Way, use the principles as guidelines and morph the exact shape to suit you. Emma demonstrates this in action. Inspiring!

Completing Step Three: Create Your Practicum Plan

Since Bright Way step three is our most detail-heavy step, I'd like to summarize as simply as possible:

- **You are your own best teacher.** Find your personal learning style. This will help you master and perform optimally. There are four learning realities that help you become your ideal instructor.
- **Your practicum plan is your personal learning and creativity template.** It has two cycles:

  Mastery => Performance Actions
  Long-Term => Daily Plans

  These interweave in spirals. Remember: *the creative path is fractal rather than linear.* Knowing this can work wonders for your confidence and energy levels! Many creatives lose a great deal of time and energy feeling upset about their progress, when they're actually spiraling beautifully.
- **Mastery is precision, while practice is flow;** both can be cultivated and are not inborn talents.
- **To add airy space to your learning and creativity,** work during your best energy times (or as close as possible to them); use the energy growing techniques I offered; and give your creativity a concrete place in your schedule.

Your practicum plan will morph over time, with each new plan being a closer match to how you want to create. What you've learned in step three is how to create a template that covers all your bases. For some, it will feel like too much detail; for others, it will be too little. Whatever you're experiencing, notice and honor it. If you need to ignore some of the more fiddly details to move forward, do so. If you need to add in your own coloratura so that you can understand the process more fully, mark up the margins of this book and incorporate supplemental materials. You are your best teacher; own this role with pride and joy.

With this new confidence and the freedom of knowing that you are your best teacher, we move to Bright Way step four, integration, where we will get to try everything on for size. I'll see you there. *You are doing the Great Work!*

You are
your best teacher;
own this role
with pride
and joy.

Step Four: Integration

Ground Your Intentions in Real Life

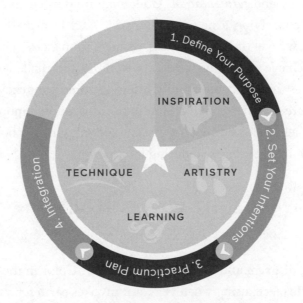

*I*ntegration comes from the Latin root for "to make whole." By making something whole, you heal it. You're about to heal your creative life, integrating skill and magic so that your dreams transmute into reality. Get ready for a very dynamic step!

During Bright Way step four, your earthy ally is technique. Technique brings grounding, structure, and physical form to your creativity. Technique entails experimenting in real life, playing in the sandbox, getting your hands dirty, and enjoying every minute. Technique can be physical and fun! We've been celebrating the mind and heart a great deal so far — let's integrate the body's deep wisdom now. Education pioneer Maria Montessori is said to have reflected on integration: "To confer the gift of drawing, we must create an eye that sees, a hand that obeys, a soul that feels; and in this task, the whole life must cooperate. In this sense, life itself is the only preparation for drawing. Once we have lived, the inner spark of vision does the rest."

Your creative process now accelerates, undergoing two alchemical operations, *conjunction* and *fermentation*. Conjunction connects everything you've done thus far, conceiving a new creative you. And in a predictable cycle, in reaching this new level of consciousness, fermentation starts. Have you noticed that once you achieve something, new opportunities and challenges appear? Fermentation shakes things up, admittedly bringing some pungency, all in the service of ever more potent creativity. Step four, integration, embodies this. It's a time of joy, closely followed by effervescent action, which is both exciting and provocative. Things get very real during integration!

BRIGHT WAY ACTIVITY
Invoke Earth ▽

Turn to the diagram at the start of this chapter. Color in the step four / technique pie piece, using whatever color invokes earth for you. Ground into this meditation, staking your creative terrain. If you have no color writing utensils, move on to part two of this activity: draw the alchemical symbol for earth (▽) inside the pie piece and down the page. Feel the downward energy of the triangle being tempered by the line, reflecting how the other elements of fire, water, air, and spirit interact with earth's mass to enliven it.

Underneath all the texts, all the sacred psalms and canticles, these watery vari-eties of sounds and silences, terrifying, mysterious, whirling and sometimes ges-tating and gentle must somehow be felt in the pulse, ebb, and flow of the music that sings in me. My new song must float like a feather on the breath of God.

— HILDEGARD OF BINGEN

Heal Yourself: Be Your Best Teacher

You've prepared for this revered role by taking the following steps:

Step one: Finding your purpose
Step two: Setting your intentions
Step three: Creating your practicum plan

Here in step four you're going to integrate all this via the direct experience of being your best teacher. Let's explore what that looks like right now.

Envision Your Best Teacher

Cast your mind back to your most inspiring, supportive, challenging, and kind teachers. What did you love about them? What did they bring forth from you? If they performed their sacred job with integrity, they opened your eyes to your vast potential and pointed the way toward manifesting it. In your Bright Way Diary, under the heading "I Am My Best Teacher," record your favorite memories.

I remember my first piano teacher, Mina Papamanolis, and her unshakable faith in me. I *knew* on a soul level that she felt I had a lot to say, plus the ability to express it. No matter how much my performance anxiety rattled me, no matter how much strife raged in the external world around me, in my inner circle with Mina, I was my true self. During my worst and most exposed moments, I called on her as my rock, someone besides my parents who believed in me un-conditionally.

Now take your beloved teacher qualities and apply them to yourself. How can you be your most inspiring, supportive, challenging, and kind teacher? How can you help yourself grow and be more yourself? You've already got the template, having just drawn up the job description. Also review the mentor recommendations section on page 34 and the four learning realities on pages 149–53.

If you have no good memories of teachers, know that you're not alone. As mentioned earlier, few people are fortunate enough to encounter their dream teacher. If this is the case for you, taking step four is even more important. Now you get to heal your relationship with learning. This is where you finally gain the teacher you've always longed for, a teacher who stays faithfully by your side, cheering you on through good and bad.

Confidence: Have Faith in Yourself

The invocational root meaning of *confidence* is "having faith in oneself." This is your prime objective now. You've been preparing for this all along by cultivating self-trust. Let's amplify self-trust so that it becomes unshakable confidence.

There's a mystery to faith that can't be explained in rational terms alone. Yes, we can employ certain factual tactics to bolster confidence, but there comes a point in your creative journey — and that moment is now! — when you must take a leap of faith and recognize other dimensions of intelligence and consciousness. It is time to conjoin mystery and practicality, light and dark, skill and magic, so that your new creative self can be born.

As you solidify your confidence in step four, integration, something astonishing emerges. Your spirit, your fifth essential element, rises. And when you finally encounter your spirit, faith in yourself becomes unquestionable reality. We'll meet the essential element of spirit full force in Bright Way step five. For now, notice whenever you experience that glimmer of recognition. It is your spirit calling.

Your Step Four Elemental Ally: Technique (Earth) ▽

We've ignited through the fire of the essential element of inspiration in step one (△).

We've flowed with the water of the essential element of artistry in step two (▽).

We've taken to the air via the essential element of learning in step three (△). Now we'll ground in earthy fertility with the essential element of technique (▽).

Bringing everything on our journey together into the physical plane, we now call on the element of earth as our natural ally. Earth represents anything that exists in the practical dimension. In the most basic terms it reflects health: your physical and mental health, the health of your life, of those around you, the health of Earth itself, all flourishing in an ecosystem of creativity. Let's ground into this consciousness.

BRIGHT WAY BREAK
Mountain Pose

Stand in the grounding yogic asana of Mountain Pose, all four corners of your feet planted firmly hip-width apart, arms hanging loosely by your sides, spine straight and proud. If this is not available to you, sit up as straight as feels comfortable, feeling rooted to your seat.

Close your eyes and meditate on how tree roots help prevent earth from eroding. Visualize energetic roots growing from your heels and fingertips, bursting through the floor and down into the earth, grounding you here in this present moment. Breathe in, focusing on your intention for today's practice. How will you use this time to root yourself more deeply in your technique? Breathe out and say aloud, "I can and I will."

Technique is the *how* of doing things. It's the craft of what you're working on. Without technique, skill is shaky. We may have ample inspiration, artistry, learning, and community, but until we transmute all these into the physical world, nothing manifests, let alone grows. Without technique, we reinvent the wheel or get stuck. Our ancestors honed technique over millennia; let us pay homage to them by refining our technical skills even further in yet another loop of Sacred Reciprocity.

With technique, things flow more smoothly and easily, allowing grace and beauty, artistry and inspiration, to infuse your creativity. Sometimes the way technique is taught makes it a joy killer. You're going to restore balance, heal, and integrate so that technique is your friend, as it always has been.

BRIGHT WAY ACTIVITY
Your Technique

Take a moment to review how technique applies to you. How does one gain skill in your field? By understanding more about gardening cycles? By auditing your chef's knife collection? By learning new ways of engaging with your children, in line with the latest discoveries of human potential and fulfillment? By mastering narrative arc more thoroughly? By documenting your findings rather than keeping everything in your head? Jot down your answers in your Bright Way Diary.

If the technical aspects of your craft are unfamiliar to you, now is an ideal moment to reach out for expert advice and community support in your specific field. Be sure to document everything in your diary.

Integrate with Earth: Your Space and Your State

We now honor the natural element of earth, refine your technique, and embody conjunction by addressing your physical situation. Two grand arenas of physical life affect your creativity: your space and your state.

Space: Your Sacred Workplace

Creative souls need a sanctuary where they connect to their source of inspiration. This sacred workspace may be an actual space or simply a state of mind. Jane Austen wrote her iconic novels on a tiny table in her noisy family drawing room. This small sanctuary fostered work that changed literature forever.

Take heart that your workspace doesn't have to be perfect — especially since there is no such thing as a perfect *anything*, let alone perfect space! Your space is always a work in progress, just like all your creative endeavors. If we get caught up in organizing the ultimate music room, the dream writing nook, the picture-perfect art corner, this can be procrastination in disguise, itself a form of fear. Bravely tend your creativity landscape now, whether it's a corner in your living room, a favorite café or library, your car, your garden, or simply a clear space inside your mind.

What's Needed in Your Space?

Comfort. You want to be able to relax in your space so that your creativity can flow. Check that your space is warm or cool enough; adequately lit; has supportive seating, shelving, or table surfaces for your essential items; room to move if needed; and any other creature comforts. Discomfort drains us, which is why decluttering has such a positive creative effect. If your home is too small or noisy, consider working in quiet public places such as libraries and cafés. Maya Angelou famously rented hotel rooms by the hour to focus on her writing. If you have no designated physical space to work in, create supportive space in your mind by harmonizing with yourself, a technique that is always available to you.

Quiet. Focus is critical for flow; it's the first part of harmonizing with yourself for this reason. Silence invites your body-mind-spirit to activate and integrate. Put your devices on airplane mode, let household members know you're entering the creative zone, and close your computer (or shut unnecessary apps). What other measures will help hone your focus? Noise-canceling headphones? Earplugs? You might also consider scheduling your creativity during quiet times in your household such as early in the morning or late at night, if either are good energy times for you. I've seen this work for musicians, where the rest of the household comes to enjoy (or at least get used to!) hearing the creative process unfold, even at the oddest hours.

Beauty. Inspiring environments stimulate creativity and motivate you to come back for more. Add little touches to enliven: a plant, a picture, flowers, a candle. Conversely, you might be more inspired by a minimalist aesthetic. Either way, create a space *you* look forward to being in, one that makes you smile and showers you with beauty. Beauty is a potent inspirational energy. Things of real beauty communicate life's truths to us. If your sacred space is mobile, finding a lovely spot in a park or taking the scenic route to your next performance space can be a tremendous boost to your energy.

Significant talismans. Meaningful items can assist in creating and holding sacred space for you, casting a safety net of love. Talismans carry intense personal energy. Examples include photos of loved ones, amulets, crystals, stones, items from childhood and significant life moments, cards, icons, statues, herbs, essences, oils, books. Our creative tools themselves — our instruments, pens, cooking utensils — sometimes play double duty as talismans. Talismans strengthen us through the energy of our most cherished relationships and beliefs. If your space is mobile, carry these items in your bag, hang them from your rear-view mirror, or screen-save them on your phone.

Add anything else to your space that calls to you. This is *your* space. Follow your imagination. Cultivating your space is a creative act in itself. As always on our Bright Way, let your space unfold organically, growing with time as you nourish it with love. Rushing and perfectionism don't work here, any more than forcing a rose to bloom would.

BRIGHT WAY BREAK
Enjoy Your Space

Sit in your new space — no matter how much or how little you have "completed" so far — drinking in its replenishing energy. What thoughts and feelings arise for you in this new space? Does it feel like it will support and expand your creativity?

State: Honor Your Earthly Self

There is one thing that when cultivated and regularly practiced, leads to deep spiritual intention, to peace, to mindfulness and clear comprehension, to vision and knowledge, to a happy life here and now and to the culmination of wisdom and awakening. And what is that one thing? It is mindfulness centered on the body.

— Buddha

Cultivating your physical state is just as important as claiming your physical space. It also pays some of the quickest learning and creativity dividends. So, how can you support your physical state?

Fuel Your Energy

Many creatives inadvertently shortchange themselves by not fueling up adequately. They run on empty, not realizing how perilously low their batteries are. The fact is, we live in physical bodies, even as we traverse wild dimensions creatively.

Getting enough sleep, eating the right foods for your body, and finding the style of movement that best suits your constitution dramatically enhance your learning and creativity. It seems curious that paying attention to mundane things could have such an effect on our magical, intuitive selves. Yet running on empty usually means we end up empty-handed, no matter how long or hard we've worked. Don't worry; the fix entails straightforward remedies, which you're about to learn, that impact your entire life for the better.

Each of us is constitutionally unique. Being your best teacher, you're going to choose what is right for *your* body. Only you can uncover what your body truly flourishes on, no matter the opinions out there regarding diet and lifestyle trends. Invest time to discover:

- how long your body needs to *sleep*
- *which foods and how much water* fuel you best
- what kind of *movement* makes sense for you — best is what you enjoy, since you'll want to keep coming back to it!

Sometimes we feel guilty about focusing on our physical needs, almost as if we're being self-indulgent. If you're struggling with this, turn back to page 135 and be recharged by Sophie's words. Any time spent on strengthening your body is time well spent, as you will experience through more fruitful learning and creativity. Love this manifestation vehicle you've been given!

BRIGHT WAY ACTIVITY
Eat with Gratitude

Honoring your state and self can be as easy as eating mindfully. As you sit down to your next meal, remember all the people, energies, and resources that went into creating your dish. Offer up a prayer of gratitude or simply say thank you to these very real entities with every bite.

By caring for your state, you allow compound benefits to blossom. Regularly practicing yoga keeps my performance energy from devolving into performance anxiety. Yoga centers me in my body, improving my rhythm. I love the aesthetic of yoga, and the beauty of alignment when it flows into place, inspiring me artistically. I also get "mat insights," ranging from brand-new notions to refinements of things I've been mulling over for ages. Sometimes they're even wholesale solutions to things I've been stuck on. You'll find me typing away in the locker room after class capturing these, many of which have found their way into this book.

Your State Assessment

Where to start in identifying your body's needs? Your state assessment is here to assist. Find a blank page in your Bright Way Diary, and divide that page into three sections. Label each section respectively "Sleep," "Sustenance," and "Movement." Then write your answers to the following questions in the corresponding sections:

Sleep. How many hours of sleep do I need to feel great? When I get enough sleep, how does this affect my learning and creativity? How is my creativity affected when I don't get enough sleep? In order to get my desired hours in, how do I need to manage my schedule? If I can't get enough hours, can I find moments to take naps and/or meditate as a makeup? If so, when? Be specific, because in itself, optimal sleep will greatly enhance your creativity.

Sustenance. How often do I need to eat in order to keep my blood sugar stable? How much water do I need to drink so that I rarely feel thirsty? How much do I need to eat before being creative so that I'm satisfied but not drowsy? What does it feel like if I eat too little or, conversely, too much? Do certain kinds of foods make me feel great throughout the day? What foods make me feel lousy as the days and weeks go by? Do I notice a difference in my learning and creating processes when I'm adequately nourished? What is my backup plan when my blood sugar has dropped too low? For example, I carry energy bars and nuts in my bag in case of emergency, and they've often been creative lifesavers.

Movement. What forms of movement are fun, beautiful, exciting, or meaningful to me: doing yoga, doing chair yoga, dancing, walking, hiking, doing tai chi, swimming, water-walking? (Going to the gym for extreme exertion is not the only option, thank goodness!) Which types of movement fit conveniently into my life? Can I combine things I enjoy, such as dancing to music I love and socializing with people I care about? Walking in botanical gardens, giving me inspiration as well as education? When can I schedule these into my day? How do I feel after I've enjoyably moved? On the other hand, how do I feel if I don't move enough? Do I get any learning and/or creativity side benefits from movement? Details matter — get earthy! Scheduling is a key point because, no matter what, our bodies eventually make us eat and sleep, but exercise is voluntary.

Your body is an ongoing creative work of art, as French philosopher Simone de Beauvoir reminds us: "The body is not a thing, it is a situation." Cultivate your body with the same joy and growth mindset (after all, you can always improve your health, no matter how incremental those changes) you approach beloved creative projects with.

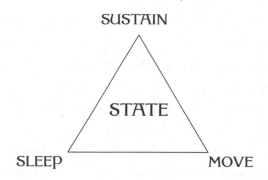

Figure 12. Your Three State Supports

BRIGHT WAY ACTIVITY
Honor Your State

Draw the "sleep-sustain-move" diagram on a sticky note and put it in your calendar. Move the note along with your schedule. This makes prioritizing your state become a habit rather than letting it remain an effort. Positive habits help you sidestep decision fatigue, self-debate, and self-sabotage. Make it as easy as possible for you to put your state on solid ground.

BRIGHT WAY BREAK
Replenish

Tending to your state, take a break now using a sleep-sustain-move replenisher, such as:

- a short nap
- a snack
- a stretch or a stroll

Discernment Instead of Judgment

Honoring physical space and state, you enter Sacred Reciprocity with them. As your space fills up with your loving attention, your body thrives. As your body thrives, you manifest ever more beauty outward.

Now let's bring Sacred Reciprocity into your relationship as your teacher-student self. It's time to integrate what at first glance appear to be polar opposites: beginner's mind and expert coach.

It's easy for us to tip into judgmental, negative states when we're acting on practically anything. Taking action is inherently risky in the sense that when you engage, you become vulnerable. Thinking rather than doing keeps us a safe distance from active engagement, from outside eyes, and from judgment.

As a Bright Way practitioner, you know that inaction drastically slows down learning and creating, ultimately leading to a life of disconnection. So action is crucial. Is there a way to take action and at the same time realistically assess how you're doing from a place of nonjudgment? Yes! It's called *discernment*.

Discernment is the ability to assess what's working and what isn't, clearly and without moral judgments. If the words *good* or *bad* come up, you're edging perilously close to judgment. Further, *good* and *bad* are vague and thus unhelpful. With discernment, *details matter*: *What* is working, and *why*? What isn't working, and why? What remedies, if any, are needed? Is something working in this context that could also be applied elsewhere? By teaching yourself with discernment, you become a master teacher. As an expert coach, you analyze with compassion and accuracy, creating an action plan moving forward.

Reflect on your favorite teachers. Were they discerning or judgmental? Imagine if they had been more judgmental: What effect might this have had on you?

> When you discern, you analyze with compassion and accuracy, and you create an action plan moving forward.

Discernment is a skill that, like all skills, you can cultivate. During integration, you'll practice discernment frequently. You *will* become expert at it. It may feel unfamiliar at first. Be patient and compassionate with yourself. Plant the seeds of discernment, and patiently allow them to take root.

Maintain beginner's mind as you uncover this new way of being. Be curious and playful as you discern. Soon discernment will become your default attitude. Harsh judgments against yourself will fade and solutions arise, as software engineer, dancer, and guitarist Holly demonstrates: "I decided not to make any value judgments on my playing, just general observations on what I was working on. I'm not a professional musician, nor do I play with other people — it doesn't matter if I'm 'good' or not. If a song was difficult or if my hands hurt, I would note that. I've found that a lot of ego / odd feelings of jealousy / 'Why am I not better at this?' sucked a lot of the joy out of dancing (certainly performing), and I wanted to keep that out of my experience with the guitar."

How to Use Discernment During Integration

Discernment directs us toward two routes:

1. **Identify what works and why.** Once you have these answers, you'll amplify the results.
2. **Identify what isn't working and why.** You'll then remedy the issues through mastery practice, postponement, or letting go with respect.

Let's find out how to walk these two routes. This is where your practicum plan reveals its power, providing the map for your actions. I offer you the following guidelines for using discernment during practice, with the caveat that you need only implement what calls to you right now. Plan on revisiting these ideas on your next turn around the spiral.

- **Lean on the Pillars of Artistry:** engage beginner's mind, be present, and deep listen throughout practice. Then:
- **When things are working for you, notice them.** Celebrate them. Pick out *how* and *why* they're working. What specific techniques did you use to succeed? What essential element actions did you take? Can you make connections between this practice session and past solutions and successes? Name your successful strategies, thereby identifying the patterns behind your learning style.
- **When things aren't working, this is valuable information, too!** It points you just as clearly toward your learning style. We know that

mistakes and struggles can be allies, encouraging us to more abundant engagement and expression. Pause and acknowledge what's really going on. Recall that you have a split second to capitalize on this learning opportunity.

Ask yourself, "*Why* isn't this working?" Rather than judging yourself, saying things such as "I'm just bad at this," or repeating what's not working over and over in the hope that it'll spontaneously improve (thereby embedding an unhelpful habit), identify the root problem. Investigate inquisitively and with the confidence that you will find the solution, in time. You will! Sometimes the solution may include a consultation with a teacher or other mentor to get additional perspective, also a decision that you initiate; the ball remains in your court as master teacher to yourself.

Here's a fun fact I've discovered: the problem is usually far smaller than we think. It's rare for whatever we're working on to be a wholesale disaster. Microscopically examining a tricky passage of music often reveals that just one awkward finger placement or one chord misunderstanding is at issue, not the entire section. Musician Teresa shares her experience of this:

"Through a fine-grained approach to discernment, I recently discovered that most of my intonation and rhythm problems on the cello mostly occur only when I'm shifting down or shifting down and crossing strings from a higher string to a lower string — the problems aren't there on the way up.

"After a couple of weeks of creating exercises to address these challenges, problems that had been holding me back for years improved in astounding ways! My teacher for more than ten years was amazed when I demonstrated the problem with the new insights and the way I was able to create a new solution."

How do we identify the root problem? This process can feel overwhelming and underwhelming at the same time. Luckily, the essential elements are here to assist once again! Filter your issue through each element, asking:

- **What inspirational needs does this problem have?** Turn to page 93 in step one to review inspiration sparks.

- **What artistic needs does this problem have?** Turn to page 115 in step two to review artistry principles.

- **What learning needs does this problem have?** Turn to page 148 in step three to review learning realities.

- **What technical needs does this problem have?** Turn to page 165 in this chapter to review technique guidelines.

- **What community needs does this problem have?** Turn to page 203 and peek ahead at step five for community-support ideas.

Act on each solution. Then assess how effective the solutions were. You know the process: log the details in your Bright Way Diary. When you know how to fix one thing, you find clues to fixing other issues as well. You diagnose problems with increased confidence, drawing on your medicine cabinet of creative remedies.

Let Go with Respect

What if the problem still doesn't dissipate? I've noticed a funny phenomenon when students are unable to master a song, even though it's within their skill level and their effort has been solid. If the song (or whatever creative endeavor you're engaged in) just won't stick, ask yourself honestly, "Do I really want to play this song?" Often, on reflection, the answer is, "Now that I think about it, I don't love this song anymore." When we don't love something, it's hard to fully master it. This is because our heart and soul are not involved. We may have the skill side covered, but there's no magic.

If you find yourself tripped up on a creative issue — a dance, a short story, a series of photographs — ask yourself this radical question: *Do I really want to do this thing?* It's okay to go a certain distance with a project and then let go of it. You will have benefited from the process simply from interacting with it. Everything is grist for the creative mill, as sculptor Auguste Rodin believed: "Nothing is a waste of time if you use the experience wisely."

It is a waste to plow on with something you don't love or need anymore. Acknowledge what you've learned from the situation, and move on graciously. Thank the situation for what it taught you. Say goodbye with respect. On the creative journey, there are infinite roads and choices; rest assured that you will have myriad alternate routes moving forward. You aren't missing out on anything. You're freeing yourself up for going places that matter to you, mind-body-spirit!

And what if you don't love the thing but you do need it? As a harpist, I've been requested to play songs I don't love for weddings and other significant events. My reframe is to go big picture: when I'm in "ceremonial musician" mode, my role is to provide the aural landscape that has most meaning for the ceremony principals. If the bride loves a certain song, if it gives her inspiration and brings her back to her true self — bingo! — I am working within my purpose of shining so that others remember who they really are. Next time you're faced with doing something that doesn't at first glance appear to align with your purpose, look again to see if there actually is a connection (remembering that this connection may play out over the long term, such as getting a degree). There won't always be a connection, but if there is, growth gold is often embedded within.

BRIGHT WAY ACTIVITY
Letting Go

At this crossroads, what are some things you can let go of with respect? What attitudes might be holding you back? What habits? Is clutter hemming you in? What do you no longer love or need? Note your answers in your Bright Way Diary. For good measure, take a pinch of salt and toss it over your left shoulder, metaphorically sloughing off old baggage.

✺　✺　✺

> # BRIGHT WAY BREAK
> ## *Refuel*

The above activity may leave you feeling a little sad, perhaps even angry that you haven't released these obstacles earlier. Be heartened: everything unfolds in its own time. Where you are is exactly where you need to be. You wouldn't be who you are today without everything that has come before. This can be hard to accept, yet when you speak with older generations, you see this knowledge shining bright in them.

Give yourself a break. Sit back and close your eyes, repeating aloud, "Everything is unfolding as it should." Allow the serenity of this attitude to ground and refuel you.

Ask for Help

What if you're stuck on something you *do* love or need? This is the moment to reach out for help. The essential element of community, which you'll learn about in depth in our next Bright Way step, is your ally at this juncture.

We all need other perspectives in order to grow. When we are lost, that's okay, because we have a solution: gather information and support. Asking for help gives you a way forward so that you are no longer stuck. Being confused and getting frustrated are temporary states. Further, they're actually helpful because they alert you that it's time to do things differently.

Asking for help is a noble thing, moving you ahead while also giving someone else the chance to feel good, cultivating Sacred Reciprocity. Often others see things we can't, illuminating blind spots. Others also help us with misattribution, meaning when we've mistakenly identified the cause of the problem. Has this ever happened to you: you thought you knew why something was amiss but someone else helped you see that a totally different thing was tripping you up? It certainly has to me!

While you are your best teacher, this doesn't mean you need to generate all information solo. How would that even be possible? If I were stuck on a desert island, I doubt I would have invented the harp, let alone mastered it in many styles. Flow with Sacred Reciprocity by gathering information from others, books, concerts, and nature, all the while keenly aware of the cornucopia of community.

BRIGHT WAY ACTIVITY
Recall Your Allies

Review your list of allies we discussed back on page 18. Turn to these allies for help now if you need it or simply to celebrate your recent creative discoveries with them.

Surveying your list, add additional sources of technical help you can call on. These could be colleagues, coaches, spiritual directors, creators whom you admire but haven't added to your circle of allies yet. Widen your skill/technique circle now.

Log Your Learning Style

By logging your creative journey, you detail your learning style. When you get specific about what is working for you, you can then amplify it. For example, do twenty-minute increments really work for you, or are longer time frames better? Do five-minute creativity sessions fit better into your life right now? Pay attention to details; these point to the patterns that make up your unique learning style. Use the integration flowchart on the next page to help you with logging.

BRIGHT WAY ACTIVITY
Picture This

Copy the integration flowchart into your Bright Way Diary. I've used a lot of words to explain the discernment process, but at the end of the day, it's simple. A picture sure is worth a thousand words!

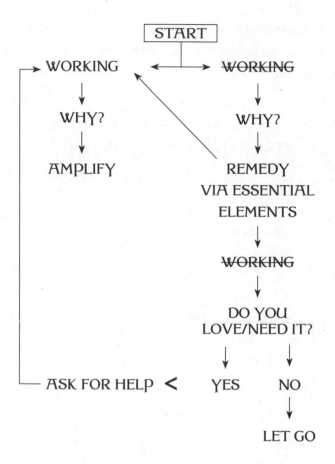

Figure 13. Integration Flowchart

BRIGHT WAY BREAK
Time to Laugh

We've been focusing on a lot of practical stuff, so it's time for a laugh! Pull up a video of a comedian you enjoy, read a funny story, watch your pets frolic. Have a good chuckle.

Integrating Performance

One of the first courses I created was Performance Mastery, which helped people transform performance anxiety into performance confidence. I developed this course from my own epic journey with stage fright, which you're familiar with by now! Even if your creative path doesn't include onstage performance, here's how I realized that performing is simply a higher-stress version of what all creatives experience on the creative journey: when you share, you perform.

> When you share, you perform.

Performing puts a magnifying glass on the creative process. Because of this, we can transpose all the principles of successful performance to any creative journey to make it more effective, motivating, convincing, and joyful.

The root word meaning of *perform* is "to carry into effect, discharge, accomplish, give form, produce." In this light, as soon as we bring the thing we've mastered into the world, we "perform" it. As we share it, it starts to interact with the world in its own right. When you share your book, you are performing. When you engage in genuine conversation, you are performing. Performing is simply sharing your engaged energy with the world.

This can feel scary. As scary as stage performance, sometimes! This is one of the reasons social anxiety is so prevalent; after all, socializing is a form of sharing and therefore a type of performing. In fact, many creatives have a feeling of being watched — of performing — throughout all stages of their work. *So let's reframe this energy as an ally instead of an enemy.*

How can we move past fear to joy and connection instead? Can we learn to share with confidence even if we've had a history of hiding, failures, and terror, as I did? You already know the answer: yes! Further, you possess the tools to share with confidence right now. The most important thing, the very foundation to sharing with love, is: know your purpose.

> The most important thing, the very foundation to sharing with love, is: know your purpose.

Yes, it all circles back to purpose! Do you remember how surprised I was to realize that purpose is the

cornerstone of creativity? Its power is miraculous. When you know your purpose and share it from your heart, suddenly performing is not about small things
like ego and approval; it's about sharing your grand message in
life.

> Be confident that
> your sharing is true,
> not contrived or
> manipulative, when
> you share from your
> purpose.

When you know your purpose, you know in your
heart why you are performing. Crucially, you feel you
have the right to take the stage in support of your message, whether in a concert hall or in quiet conversation with a friend. Magically, in turn, your purpose
resonates with others, inviting them to share their true
selves as well.

The word *performing* sometimes takes on the pejora-
tive meaning of being fake. Cast your mind back to performances that moved you. Were they fake? The hallmark of a moving performance
is that it rings true. Be confident that your sharing is true, not contrived or
manipulative, when you share from your purpose.

Practicing Performance

Following the power of purpose, my second biggest performing surprise was
realizing that performance can be practiced. Performing is — you know it! — a
skill you can build. In Bright Way step three we discussed the difference between
mastery and performance, and I promised to share my performance flow guidelines. Here they are.

Normalize Sharing (Performing)

Many of us were terrified when we started driving. Back then, we were conscious of every move, grimly aware of the consequences of any mistake. Now
we sometimes arrive places without even being aware of how we got there. What
changed? Simply this: we practiced driving often enough to make it normal.
Normalization can turn something harrowing to something earthly. Let's use
normalization to make performing second nature for you as well.

The fact is that driving can be extremely dangerous. However, performing your art is unlikely to be lethal. I think we creatives all need to be reminded once in a while that performing is not a life-and-death scenario!

What are some safe ways to perform in low-stakes situations, giving you plenty of practice without negative consequences? Try out the following ideas, many of which apply whether you are playing music, reading your writing out loud, showing your artwork, having a heart-to-heart conversation, meeting new people, cooking for guests, or engaging in any other kind of sharing:

- **Perform to your phone's video camera.** Doing this replicates the performance setting strikingly well. You don't even have to watch the video if you don't want to. The key is to get used to having an "eye" on you. Over time you start to realize you can control that eye no more than you could control an audience. This frees you up to focus on what you're doing and not be distracted.
- **Perform for friends.** Make a date to share your work with each other, either in person or online. This exposure makes performing a natural thing you do, and you cultivate joy and community while you're at it!
- **Perform in public spaces where you're in the background, not in the spotlight.** Parks, public lobbies, libraries, schools, animal shelters, farmers' markets, nonprofits, coffeehouses, retirement homes: there are thousands of places that would welcome your art. Get imaginative, and look around your environment for opportunities to share.

BRIGHT WAY ACTIVITY
Share Your Creativity

Brainstorm where and how you can share your creativity. After a while it will become normal to perform, an everyday celebration of life itself. You'll also be hearing many ways to share creativity throughout this chapter.

Performance Flow

One of our Bright Way mantras is "Mastery is precision, performance is flow." When we flow, we carry on, no matter what happens. And the unexpected will happen, guaranteed! Can we prepare for the unexpected? Yes: experiment with these flow-enhancing, resilience-building techniques:

- **Practice going through your entire presentation, with no stops.** During mastery practice, we focus intently on just a few aspects of our work. With performance, we string everything together, delivering it in one go. This requires stamina; otherwise we can run out of steam alarmingly fast. Practice your entire presentation without stopping: you'll build stamina by learning to manage your energy more efficiently. You'll get the artistry bonus of seeing how the arc of your work holds together. You may find opportunities to edit your work so that it's even more powerful. Writers sometimes do this by reading aloud, adding a new dimension to their work (something I tried and loved while writing this book).

- **Practice making mistakes and recovering from them.** Airline pilots spend most of their training learning how to deal with challenges, malfunctions, and errors. When it's actual performance time for them, the stakes are too high not to know how to recover. Further, as we know, mistakes in all their various permutations ("volunteer" notes, memory lapses, missteps, incorrect technique, accidents such as broken strings and gear, to name a few of the myriad bungles we're prone to) are inevitable. Specific examples of creative "mistakes" include deliberately playing the wrong chord in a song, allowing your brush to drag the wrong way in a painting, and having a character say or do something unplanned in your writing.

  Knowing that you can recover is a massive relief and a confidence booster. My greatest performance fear was not being able to recover from mistakes and therefore having to leave the stage — a fear that came true, as you heard! Learning how to improvise helped me get over the idea that every single note needed to be in a precise place and also gave me the tools to extrapolate on the fly. Not to mention, improvisation opened up a whole world of arranging and composing to me. What does improvising look like in your field? If you're not doing it already, make improvisation part of your practice. Its benefits deserve a book of their own!

So, deliberately make mistakes. (Choose any from the short list above or make new ones — there's certainly no shortage of options.) and find ways to get back on track. You'll feel a million times better when real showtime comes around, knowing you've got escape hatches identified left and right.

BRIGHT WAY ACTIVITY
Prepare for the Unexpected

How can you prepare for the unexpected in order to sustain and/or generate creative flow in your performance? How have your feelings about making mistakes evolved on our journey together? Do you believe that a mistake doesn't have to be a catastrophe? Can mistakes be a form of composting, creating more fertile ground for future learning and creativity? As Thich Nhat Hanh reminds us, we can't have the lotus without the mud. Perhaps you even got some additional inspirational or learning ideas? Please note your reflections in your Bright Way Diary.

Maintaining a Loving Performance Mindset

As you integrate your creativity with the world — whether from stages or in kitchens — I offer the following six positive performance mindsets. These perspectives have all been extensively road tested and apply to almost any creative activity. Let's consider each in detail.

Performance Energy Is Your Ally, Not Your Enemy

When I returned to music, desperate to finally conquer my performance anxiety, I heard a lot about "squashing" this "enemy." A famous musician advised me not to give anxiety an inch, to fight it tooth and nail. I heard that I should throw up a "shield" against the fear by playing in my own little "bubble."

These approaches are doomed to failure. By entering into battle with performance anxiety, I gave it strength. Just like focusing on the negative makes things worse, the more I railed against stage fright, the craftier it got. I eventually resorted to taking beta-blockers (note: these are only to be taken with a prescription) to cut my adrenaline surges. They helped me in numerous ways, and I'm grateful for them. They taught me what it felt like to be onstage without a panic attack looming. They helped me preserve my energy before performances by keeping me from shaking four thousand calories an hour away. And here's the best thing: they taught me that adrenaline is my ally.

Adrenaline helps you be superhuman in the sense that you rise above your regular state. This creates greater focus, alertness, and magnetism. Your reaction time shortens. You become larger than life. These factors all enhance performance. Without them your performance — your very engagement — becomes flat and uninspired.

This is how I finally understood that *managing* performance energy is the secret to neutralizing stage fright. Performance energy is hugely helpful *and must be controlled by you.* Learning to manage your performance energy is completely possible, as you have learned throughout our journey.

Audiences Want to Feel

"What people really want is to feel something, not be impressed." So said Roy, my piano teacher whom you met earlier, as he tried to comfort my distraught self before a big performance. Between my tears, his words started to sink in. Why do people come to concerts, after all? Some people may want to be awed or to see something flashy, but in the end, don't they really want to feel something? To be touched in their hearts and souls? Yes: I believe that they want confirmation of their existence. They want to know they're not alone and that we're all mysteriously connected on this magnificent, perplexing journey together. They want to know there's someone who understands what they feel and who resonates in sympathy.

When you're sharing your work, remember Roy's words. It's easy to get caught up in hoping that others will notice how exceptional our work is and admire our efforts. Yet that's all a sideshow to the main event. Primarily our audiences want to *feel*, and this feeling happens with the simplest to the most complex of materials. Think back to a modest song, image, or phrase that moved you. What distinguishes it is not how difficult it was; it's the energy with which it was created and shared. Share from your purpose: that energy is true.

> Share from your purpose: that energy is true.

Your Creativity Is Not Your Identity

Performing can feel like putting your soul on trial. However, as mentioned earlier, your creativity is not your identity. Your products and process are not the final words on the state of your soul. And they're definitely not actual pieces of your soul! They're simply reflections of you, a moment in time, sharing where you are right now.

When you share from the heart, you also hold the mirror up to your audience. They have a chance to reflect on themselves. I remember Roy telling me, "Diana, people in the audience aren't thinking about you. They're thinking about themselves and their lives." Give your audience this space. Don't waste energy or interfere by trying to control them in any way. Just focus on sharing in the most direct and heartfelt way you can. That is enough.

> Focus on sharing in the most direct and heartfelt way you can. That is enough.

Treat Yourself Kindly, As You Would Others

When you perform, think about how you treat others, and remember to treat yourself with that same kindness and consideration. When you're performing, you're being brave. Acknowledge that, no matter how the performance goes. Later, you can review what worked and what didn't, but that's going back to mastery.

When you're in performance mode, stay there. Let it flow, let it be what it is, and above all, let it come from the heart, both for your audience and yourself.

Vulnerability Is Power

When you share from the heart, you are being vulnerable. You lower your shields and reveal your truth. Truth is power that stands the test of time. Truth may get perverted and co-opted, but in the end, the truth will out. As Aristotle wrote, "With the truth, all given facts harmonize; but with what is false, the truth soon hits a wrong note."

You have nothing to fear by telling your heart's truth and therefore being vulnerable. In fact, you wield the power of the universe by connecting to your mighty truth. Remember this when you start feeling small or worried about sharing your reality. Stand strong in your courageous vulnerability. And call on Sacred Reciprocity to ensure that you're sharing from a place of life affirmation and the intention to connect in love.

Time Is Also Your Ally

On the Bright Way, your relationship with time will start to warm and expand. Besides realizing that everything you've done up to this moment has brought you to where you are now — which is exactly the right place to be! — you'll find as we walk this journey that time starts to behave differently. Where you might once have regretted "lost time," you'll find that you are not behind, that you don't have to "catch up," and that you haven't "missed out." Everything is unfolding as it should, and time is on your side.

> Everything is unfolding as it should, and time is on your side.

As you grow in skill, you learn more thoroughly and more quickly, so your technique grows exponentially. As you embrace your magic, your inspiration and artistry bloom in ways you never dreamed of. Blasts of insight gift you with what seem like years of wisdom, instantly. Where you once struggled to make progress or find motivation, they become second nature to you. Time expands: you have more time to create and, paradoxically, you find time flying by as you live joyously.

And those moments when you feel tired? Time is also your

ally, not your enemy, because it is recommending you now switch tasks. Cycling between states of high and low intensity, you gain long-term endurance and keep your inspiration topped off. Getting stuck in high gear will surely burn you out, as I know from personal experience. When time comes down on me and says, "Okay, time for a break!," it is in fact protecting me. Without time's prodding, I might easily spend twelve hours on the same task for days on end, which will certainly not play out for the best in the long run, either for my skill or my magic. All the research is in: taking a break improves just about every aspect of your learning and creativity.

Some say that time isn't a real dimension and that it's simply because we're on an earthly plane that we experience this illusion. Given that our elemental ally for integration is earth, it is fitting that time comes into play most here in Bright Way step four. Explore the edges of your relationship with time, both positive and negative, each time (!) you practice.

BRIGHT WAY ACTIVITY
Pick a Mindset

List the six performance mindsets, detailed above, in your Bright Way Diary. Pick one mindset to ground you over the next few days. Dwell on its teachings. How can you put these teachings into practice? Make note in your diary.

Completing Step Four: The Big Picture of Integration

We've taken a big step together, and no wonder: you're integrating your creative ecosystem! During step four, you:

- Live your purpose and intentions via your practicum plan, powered into manifestation by your skill and magic.
- Take on the mantle of being your own teacher, integrating your personal learning style into your daily life.
- Support your learning style in the physical world by crafting a sacred workspace and fueling yourself sustainably.

- Learn how to perform — share! — your creativity from a place of love, not fear.
- Realize that time is on your side and that you are right where you need to be.
- Notice how all things in life converge into one great ocean of creative engagement. Talk about integration!

And speaking of picturing integration, take a look at the diagram below. Does it reflect your integration journey?

WHAT WE THINK IT SHOULD LOOK LIKE:

WHAT IT FEELS LIKE:

WHAT IT ACTUALLY IS:

Figure 14. The Creative Journey: Three Perspectives

BRIGHT WAY ACTIVITY
The Fractal of Creativity

Draw the Creative Journey diagram in your Bright Way Diary. Note any feelings and reflections that come up for you.

Now let's celebrate your achievements in Bright Way step five: fulfillment, the most fun and yet the most underestimated step of all. Step five sets you up to maintain the integration of your passion, focus, and momentum. This crucial final step ensures that all your hard work pays off forever.

Come join your party!

Step Five: Fulfillment

Your Ongoing Creative Story:
Joy and Resilience in Sacred Reciprocity

You've made it! You've reached the final milestone of this turn of the spiral, step five: fulfillment. Fueled by purpose, you've worked and played with intention. You've ridden the ups and downs of daily practice. Best of all, you've forged a whole new relationship with your creativity and with your life. Now, like a farmer resting comfortably in the plentitude of her harvest, it is time to reflect and toast the fulfillment of your purpose. It's time to celebrate *you*.

Take a look at our unified wheel above, flowing in its intertwined cycles of engagement and creativity. As you glance at each step and each essential element, recall your progress, your joys, and your victories. Later in this step you'll get to revel fully — this is just a preview of what's to come.

Smile and nod in agreement with your unabashedly proud feelings. It's a radical act in our culture to pause and genuinely appreciate your efforts and — gasp! — your achievements *for yourself*. You've traveled so far, learned so much, and given so much, all in Sacred Reciprocity. You deserve this moment in the sun. Salute yourself for having made it through the struggles and learned from your mistakes. Perhaps especially, acknowledge yourself for having the strength to sit with what remains unknown. For there is still much to be discovered on your creative path! Guided by the shining wisdom of your heart, you've achieved much and have much to look forward to.

It's at this point that you might feel your spirit most strongly. Perhaps you already have a close relationship with your spirit, perhaps it's more of a sixth-sense feeling for you, maybe it's a perception of life force coursing vividly through you. Other names for spirit include *pneuma*, *qi*, *prana*, *rauch*, *quintessence* (giving a nod to spirit as our fifth element!). Spirit is a very personal experience. Whatever you are feeling is fitting for you.

BRIGHT WAY ACTIVITY
Invoke Spirit O

Turn to the diagram at the start of this chapter. Color in the step five / community pie piece, using whatever color invokes spirit for you. Feel uplifted and fulfilled by this meditation. If you have no color writing utensils, move on to part two of this activity: draw the alchemical symbol for community (O) inside the pie piece and up the page. Feel the circular, complete, and spiraling energy of spiritual connection.

✷ ✷ ✷

You now advance to *distillation* and *coagulation*, the crowning alchemical operations of this Great Work. Distillation comes first, reflecting the refined results of all your efforts, the clarifying of what your journey has really been about. This potent proof leads you to coagulation. What a word! It may conjure up the image of a healing wound for you. It speaks truth: you have undertaken an epic journey of healing. Returning to your true self, you have reclaimed your true power. You are the hero of this story. Now is your triumphant return home.

Alchemical iconography depicts coagulation as the marriage of a king and queen. This represents bringing together male/female, active/receptive, dark/light archetypal energies. The root meaning of *fulfillment* is "to consummate, to complete, to bring into effect." You have coupled many energies on your Bright Way path, all in service to your soul's message, your purpose. You know body-mind-spirit that what appear to be opposites are merely at different ends of the same pole. By integrating these opposites, you allow these poles to intertwine and strengthen as the backbone of your creative life.

Figure 15. The Creative Caduceus

Ultimately, fulfillment celebrates the grand marriage of yourself to your Self — and, by extension, to the great cosmos of which we are all a part. You've integrated your skill and magic, your heaven and earth, and perhaps most important, your body and spirit into your uniquely creative soul.

BRIGHT WAY ACTIVITY
Spirals

Draw the diagram above in your Bright Way Diary. As you do, meditate on what you sense as the spirals intertwine around the pole. What do these spirals and the pole represent to you and your creative journey? Perhaps skill and magic in service to manifestation (resulting in performance and/or presentation)? Light and dark in service of truth (such as honoring Bright Knowledge as well as mysterious intuition)? Healing, as in the caduceus? DNA? Spiral learning? Note your reflections in your diary.

Fulfillment Is a Real Step

If you're feeling reluctant to spend time tooting your own horn, let me reassure you that fulfillment has an enormous effect on your creative process. In my experience teaching the Bright Way and by personal observation throughout my life, it is also by far the most overlooked step. *To be completely up-front, without owning this step, your creativity does not just regenerate.* Without practicing fulfillment, you cannot attain sustainable creativity.

> **Without practicing fulfillment, you cannot attain sustainable creativity.**

Most people want to skip or skim past this step. They fear it's selfish to celebrate themselves. They fear becoming arrogant. They fear losing momentum in a sea of self-indulgence. Perhaps you're itching to get to the finish line as well? Here's the thing: all these are fear-based feelings (plus, and most important, there is no finish line). As we've learned on our journey together, fear is creativity's opponent. Forget fear! Celebrate with joy, beam love to yourself, and shine it on all of us. Joy is the greatest motivator.

Yet sometimes we may also fear joy. The inevitable swing of the pendulum means we can't constantly feel joyful. Fulfillment is actually its own remedy: as you expand your capacity to feel joy and celebrate the abundance that is your creative life, you become polarized in positivity. Your default perspective becomes optimism rather than pessimism. Your benchmark for joy rises, and you both notice and attract more positivity into your life on all levels. Yes, you will still absolutely experience the rhythm of change — there will be bad days, disappointments, and stresses — but your personal pendulum will swing over a landscape of positivity rather than one of gloomy limitation.

Alchemy shows us that this final step is the pinnacle of this cycle. It can't be ignored. If we don't honor it, then like all things that get squashed down or overlooked, it will wither or pervert. Honor yourself, and you will find it easier to honor others. Judge yourself, and it's a short step toward living in judgment of others, too.

Fulfillment is vital for myriad reasons, the most key of which we'll examine in this chapter. Yet the step itself is all about fun and celebration. You have worked for this moment. You deserve it. Let your hair down, relax. It's your party!

> *"Come on, Zorba," I cried, "teach me to dance!"*
> *Zorba leaped to his feet, his face sparkling.*
> *"To dance, boss? To dance? Fine! Come on!"*
> *"Off we go, then, Zorba! My life has changed! Let's have it!"*
>
> — NIKOS KAZANTZAKIS, *Zorba the Greek*

How to Practice Fulfillment, First Pass

Take out your Bright Way Diary and under the heading "I Am Fulfilled," write down all the achievements you've enjoyed during this first spiral of our journey. Refer back to previous pages in your diary to spark memories. Look through your calendar, emails, and cards that loved ones have sent you. Meditate on our wheel. Look around your sacred workspace, at the pen atop a stack of papers, the open string set lying here, the scribbled-on sticky note...

I've walked hundreds of people through this process, and let this fact encourage you: never once have I experienced anyone being disappointed by this step, even the people who resisted it at first! They have all reported that they can hardly believe all they've achieved. Dave Mahony, whom we met back in Bright Way step one (I've found writers among the most recalcitrant when it comes to doing written Bright Way exercises!) said:

> "I couldn't have been less thrilled when Diana told me to write down a list of my accomplishments. Ugh. The horror! Can you imagine? If only she'd asked me for a list of failures. That, I could do.
>
> "So when I sit down to try and write the dang list, to somehow manage to come up with one single victory in the miserable wreck that is my creative life, I manage to do it. One. Huzzah!
>
> "But then I squeak out another. And another. And before I know it, the list is getting longer and longer. Victories I'd ignored, forgotten, or just plain missed are popping up like gophers in the lawn.
>
> "Some days the victory was simply getting up in the morning. Some victories were big — I had managed to sell an actual screenplay in Hollywood, after all. But seen among the constellation of achievements both big and small, each one gained a new significance."

As you write down your victories, feel them. Relive them in full color. They may be small. They may be large. Judging your victories is not what this is about. The important thing is to feel them, wholeheartedly. Let the process unfold. It will take on a life of its own.

This all may feel strange at first. Stay with it. Practice it. You're expanding your faith, love, and hope in yourself. You're growing and evolving.

Take inspiration from nature once more. Is a rainbow ashamed of its beauty? Does a flower underplay its loveliness? Does thunder hold back? Celebrate your magnificence! Hiding your joy is like being a bird with its wings clipped. Free yourself!

Fulfillment is a creative act, not a holding pattern. During this step you *actively* celebrate the successes *you* made happen on our journey. I'll say it again: no victory is too small. Don't underestimate your achievements. Make an effort to remember that it's often those tiny seeds of achievements that become enormous redwoods in the long term. Practice the humble realization that we don't know everything; we don't know how things will turn out. Give every win its place. Cherish every joy, every hurdle overcome, every inspired thought, every mistake recognized, every connection made, every ally honored, every single piece of progress you made happen.

As you document, relive, and embed your triumphs in your consciousness, your confidence strengthens. You may not notice it much at first. Trust that you've planted the seeds. Or maybe you'll be hit like a bolt of lightning, suddenly fired up with unshakable faith in yourself. All is well, and one way is not better than another. Whatever happens for you is what is meant to happen.

Tap It In!

Read your fulfillment list. Feel joy coursing through your body-mind-spirit. Now embed that joy deeper into these dimensions by tapping between your eyebrows, a technique we learned in Bright Way step one on page 98.

Besides heightening and embedding positive emotions, "tapping it in" also builds resilience, a key ally on our creative path. You need to make an important call? Tap between your eyebrows and recall previous positive feelings you've embedded, emboldening you with confidence. It's a conditioned response you can count on.

This new confidence perfectly positions you for your next level of creativity. Yet there's no need to rush ahead. Let's inhabit in this step, rallying our allies for even more support and celebration, before the wheel turns and your new horizons dawn.

Fulfillment: Finally Believing in Yourself

When we started our journey together, I spoke about the fact that many people suffer from Impostor Syndrome. They feel like frauds, unworthy of living a creative existence. For a million and one reasons, many people feel they don't deserve to have a creative life. They feel it's not their place to engage creatively with life, that they just don't "have it." You might even have felt this way at the start of our journey. You know how much I felt that way, and for how long.

I'll say it: *people feel unworthy because they haven't internalized their successes.* They don't own their successes body-mind-spirit. They downplay victories as flukes and thus fear being exposed at any moment. Living in this constant state of low-level fear drains their life force. I don't want this to happen to you. I want you to see yourself in your true radiance! Yet it doesn't matter what I want: *you have to want this for yourself.*

You have to want this for yourself.

All the positive external feedback in the world adds up to a molehill if you don't actually believe that *you* are the reason your achievements have come to light. Plus, others' positive feedback may not acknowledge what we most value on our creative journey. Have you been complimented on something you considered tangential to your creativity, leaving you disappointed that you heard nothing about the thing you cared about most? Even lovely comments can backfire if we rely on feedback to validate us. Here is the most important message I can impart to you: the only person who can truly make you believe in yourself is you.

Even those who have the highest academic, artistic, and business-related achievements suffer from feelings of unworthiness. Shouldn't public recognition automatically make people feel good about themselves? Yet so often it doesn't, and they don't. What's it going to take? Winning an Oscar? There are many miserable Oscar winners. Climbing Mount Everest? Fine, but what do you do when there are no higher mountains to conquer? Here's a horrifying thought: If someone we look up to feels like a failure in secret, are we chasing illusions, too? What if all our creative engagement will come to naught? *Have we come this far for nothing?*

I used to think that if only I achieved that next goal, got those kudos from that musician I admired, received that positive review, then I would finally feel okay. Yet when these wishes were granted, it wasn't long before I slipped back to my old baseline of feeling scared and undeserving. It was maddening. Why couldn't I just feel better? Now I know what was going on: *I never dared to be fulfilled.* I never allowed myself to say "nice job!" to myself. And this seemingly small act is crucial if we are to lead joyful, creative lives.

Telescope back to observe: you fulfill Sacred Reciprocity of the entire Bright Way System by celebrating your work, effort, and play. Let's bring home why fulfillment is essential to your creative life.

Love Yourself, Love Life, Love Others

By believing in yourself, you come to love yourself sincerely with innocence and humility, embodying the wonder that is beginner's mind. And aren't we all beginners in this great university of life?

Fulfillment shows us that, if you want to love, you must start by loving yourself first. And As Above, So Below: by loving yourself, your feelings radiate out to include those around you and, by extension, the entire world. Here's the amazing thing: you don't even have to try! In fact, don't try; just shine like the sun, and we all will feel it. We want to feel your love; we need your love. Here it is: *we need to feel your connection*. And it starts with you loving yourself, which fulfillment facilitates.

As you appreciate yourself, you appreciate others more. You become brave and more willing to show them how you feel. This helps them blossom, and in turn, everyone grows. As you fall back in love with yourself, so you fall in love with the world again.

> The only person who can truly make you believe in yourself is you.

I've seen this happen countless times. My friend and collaborator, singer Jennifer Paulino, excitedly shared her recent teaching breakthrough with me. When she privately centered in love, using a method similar to harmonizing with yourself, *before* her students arrived, her students automatically began singing better. They easily hit notes they previously strained for. Their expression became direct and impassioned. When Jennifer focused on the big picture — *connection* — incredibly, the practical details fell into place, too. This is what fulfillment looks like in real life.

When I first practiced fulfillment, things also began aligning for me. I gained faith that I could reach out further, take bigger risks, trust more, make mistakes and recover, create more. My performances improved. Previously, I used to go onstage wordlessly, recite each piece without comment, bow, and exit. I was too scared to speak! Gaining confidence through fulfillment, I realized, "Wait a minute, I *want* to share what this song means to me and where it came from." Now chatting with my audience is a hallmark of my performances. This has made for much more intimate, moving, and memorable events, if I say so myself, and I recommend you give it a try, too. Talk about finding your voice!

My teaching also improved. I no longer worried about my students getting freaked out about making mistakes. We both laughed heartily over goofs and bonded over performance war stories. "Mistakes" got put in their proper place as allies, not enemies.

Fulfillment: Antidote to Burnout, Elixir of Creativity

Even if you already believe in yourself, pausing and reflecting with satisfaction on your achievements is crucial. If you don't take a moment to slow down and bask in the pleasure of what you have achieved, burnout will eventually exact its toll. Trudging from goal to goal without pause, people often end up feeling like a machine churning out products, without any vision of process. And we all know where that leads.

Just as the seasons must change to keep the earth habitable, we change our creative cycles to maintain our health. This counts for our health on all levels: physical, mental, emotional, spiritual, and even social. It might seem fun to stay in that "perfect summer day" mode forever. Yet eventually everything would diminish and die without rain. Switch creative seasons. This is what wise stewardship of your creative energy looks like. During this period of introspection, allow your fields to lie fallow so that your creative nutrients can replenish.

Marking this season of our journey with a celebration is most fitting. From invitation to initiation and through all the steps, fulfillment completes this trip around the spiral. Fulfillment is a rite of passage. You've made it! Celebrate! A new creative era is about to dawn for you.

How to Practice Fulfillment, Second Pass

Knowing all that you now know about fulfillment, please go back and reread what you wrote regarding your achievements. How do you feel? Do you want to add anything? Take anything away? Make notes in your Bright Way Diary.

Your Step Five Elemental Allies: Community (Spirit) O

We've ignited through the fire of the essential element of inspiration in step one (△).

We've flowed with the water of the essential element of artistry in step two (▽).

We've taken to the air via the essential element of learning in step three (△̵).

We've grounded in earthy fertility with the essential element of technique in step four (▽̵).

Now, in step five, we connect and enliven all with spirit and community (O).

Looking back on your journey, you may realize that an invisible force like gravity, a benevolent, all-pervading spirit, has been allied with you this entire time. It has quietly waited in the wings, providing unsaid, unconditional love through times good and bad. This spirit has infused your path with meaning beyond words.

This spirit is your true self. You are this spirit. And it also exists all around you as sheer life force. This spirit is *connection*. It is community: the communing of life-affirming forces gathered in service to love.

Early in our creative journeys, we often want to be original or disruptive. I understand; we want to make our mark, to be seen, to share something of indisputable value. Here's the thing; *you* are that thing of unique value. Everything already exists in our universe as raw materials. We're all playing with these same materials, recycling them in new ways to

> The only truly original thing is *you, your soul.* You shine in our world as a one-time marriage of body and spirit that will never be exactly replicated. Your precious soul engages with life creatively, affecting all it interacts with: this is your most powerful contribution to life.

reflect new times. Trying to be completely original is an illusion. The only truly original thing is *you, your soul.* You shine in our world as a one-time marriage of body and spirit that will never be exactly replicated. Your precious soul engages with life creatively, affecting all it interacts with: this is your most powerful contribution to life. And while it may seem too large to catch hold of, your soul has an embodiment that guides you reliably in the real world: your purpose.

> *You turn the wheel and the mud whirls round, as if you were possessed while you stand over it and say: I'm going to make a jug, I'm going to make a plate, I'm going to make a lamp and the devil knows what more! That's what you might call being a man: freedom!*
>
> — NIKOS KAZANTZAKIS, *Zorba the Greek*

BRIGHT WAY ACTIVITY
Connect the Heart and Mind

At first glance, our journey has been about bringing together skill and magic. We have learned how to marry practicality and intuition so that we can manifest — create — more meaningfully. Ultimately, this journey is about the marriage of your body-mind-spirit so that you become whole once again.

Let's celebrate with this exercise: place one hand on your heart and the other at your third eye (the space between your eyebrows). Breathe. Scan your body for any energy blockages. Breathe into any tight spots. Feel present and comfortable. Now bring your attention back to your hands connecting your heart and head. Do you feel your heart and mind communicating? Do you feel sparkling energy bouncing back and forth between them, the communing of heart and head? I believe this is one of the best ways to sense your spirit physically. How does this feel for you? What emotions does this bring up? Look again at the figure on page 195. Do you notice any additional connections coming up for you? Make note in your diary.

❖   ❖   ❖

How Spirit and Community Connect

Spirit's unseen energy infuses our creativity with life force. When we let our spirit flow into our work, everything connects and comes to life. Our work goes beyond even skill, magic, and manifestation, to the transcendent.

Community also often goes unrecognized as foundational to creativity. Like spirit, community can elevate our creativity to something universal, timeless. Before we get into the details of how community lights up the creative path, let's experience the feeling of community first via the following Bright Way Activity. After all, both spirit and community reside in the realm of the mystical in that they must be directly experienced in order to be understood.

BRIGHT WAY ACTIVITY
The Mutual Gaze

Stand or sit facing a trusted friend or creative partner. Set a timer for five minutes. You and your partner now look into each other's eyes in a mutual gaze. Maintain eye contact. Allow anything to run through your mind, such as musings about time, thoughts about how weird this activity feels, a realization of your partner's true eye color. Keep gentle eye contact. Practitioners of this mutual gaze have experienced powerful emotions, redeeming tears, occasional hallucinations, and warmth wash over them. And no wonder; you're communing with the spirit of your beloved person! If this feels too intense for you right now, that's fine. Simply experiment with making eye contact with others more often.

Community in Fulfillment:
Gratitude, Connection, and Collaboration

Sometimes people worry that celebrating themselves will somehow set them apart from others or perhaps even cut them off from community. We've all heard the "tall poppy gets cut" admonishment.

Celebrating your achievements does not look like bragging. In fact, you may choose to celebrate quietly to yourself as you write out your accomplishments and smile in acknowledgment and ownership of them. Perhaps you'll choose to share your findings with close friends, and perhaps more widely.

Here's the magical thing: as you genuinely own your achievements, you come to *greater appreciation* of the forces that helped you get there. You are grateful when you recall the faces of all who have supported and inspired you, the towering figures from the past who laid the way for you today, all your allies. Rather than cultivating smugness, celebrating your achievements opens the door to honoring others. You realize how much of your creativity is built on those who came before you, as well as those around you right now. In Sacred Reciprocity you recognize all the allies who have quietly supported you. You connect with the Bright Knowledge in the deepest way, becoming one with it.

Before I accepted that I am — as you are! — part of the Bright Knowledge, I used to be terrible about accepting compliments, brushing them off like flies. I'd deflect, telling the other person how much better they were than me, that my accomplishment was no big deal, and I'd speculate on its imminent demise. Then one day a friend burst out in frustration: "When I give you a compliment and you blow it off, it's an insult. You're throwing my gift away. I want to give this gift. I want you to enjoy it. *I want to feel good about giving it, and you're denying me that.* Just take it, already!"

This is Sacred Reciprocity: someone gives, and you give in return. Remember how you felt last time you gave someone a gift they loved? Didn't you feel wonderful, perhaps just as wonderful as the recipient?

BRIGHT WAY ACTIVITY
Accepting Compliments

When people compliment you, practice accepting their gift with gratitude. This doesn't have to look dramatic; just smile sincerely and say thank you. Believe they mean what they say, with no ulterior motives.

Stay relaxed and comfortable during this process — this lets your admirer know they've made you feel happy, not awkward. Receive the loving energy coming to you. Reflect it back in Sacred Reciprocity.

We've discovered that fulfillment stokes the all-powerful state of gratitude, one of the most positive emotions we can experience. Some even believe it's the secret to happiness. As a massive bonus, it's practically impossible to feel fear when we feel grateful. Gratitude means we live from a place of love. And as we've learned on our journey, creativity is love — *connection* — made manifest. Love and creativity feed each other in a loop of Sacred Reciprocity.

BRIGHT WAY ACTIVITY
Compliment Someone

Gratitude, connection, and collaboration can all be practiced in one fell swoop via one of my favorite ways to cultivate community: compliment someone on their creative work. It doesn't have to be anything major; perhaps mention how much you enjoyed a well-crafted email, a funny joke, a beautiful meal, or simply being heard. As you practice gratitude, feel your collaboration flow. Try this sweet practice now.

How We Spiral Together: You Are Not Alone

Feeling gratitude for all who have contributed to creating this book, I ponder, where do I end and they begin? What is "mine" and what is someone else's starts to overlap. This is a beautiful thing! As I mentioned, there's nothing new in this universe except our creative souls. I don't own any of this except my own voice, my own creativity. And that is more than enough!

As I call on the Bright Knowledge for inspiration, I am grateful to our ancestors, our ancient communities, and I know in my bones that they are part of me. As I watch my students grow, I am humbled to see that I've become part of them. My student Susan says, "You will always be a part of my life and mindset. Whether it's following your philosophy or doing yoga exercises, practicing, writing in my harp journal and my daily gratitude book, there you are! Your voice and persona are a part of me now."

Are we ever really alone? We may feel disconnected, *but that's an illusion.* We can't help but be connected. We "inter-are," Thich Nhat Hanh elaborates, connected in infinite ways across infinite dimensions. We exist and function due to the seen and unseen assistance of many others. Yet many people feel lonely. They feel isolated and believe they struggle alone. We know this pain is real. How can we feel our connection again? How can we realize that we are in fact already deeply connected?

> When we directly engage in life — *by being creative* — all the connections *that already exist* illuminate.

When we directly engage in life — *by being creative* — all the connections *that already exist* illuminate. We find ourselves in community again, and mysteriously, we discover it's where we've been all along. The illusion is that we were ever separated. We recognize we are one, and our spirits are restored. And so we create abundantly in order to celebrate connection in our world.

BRIGHT WAY ACTIVITY
Spirit, Community, Life Force

Trace the diagram from page 195 that you drew in your Bright Way Diary, now sensing the intertwining spirals as representing spirit and community and the straight line as representing life force. What reflections come up for you? Note these in your diary.

❖ ❖ ❖

Cultivating Community

As creatives, we all need a real, supportive community to mirror, encourage, and challenge us. Van Gogh knew he had something brilliant to share with the world, and it was torture for him that few reflected that fact back to him. Yes, we strengthen from the inside first, bolstering our internal power and identifying our purpose. Yet we are also fueled by Sacred Reciprocity with the world around us, and need this energy to feel fully alive.

> We are fueled by Sacred Reciprocity with the world around us, and we need this energy to feel fully alive.

It is now time in our journey together to reintegrate the external, this time from a place of internal strength. Your inner and outer spaces are ready to marry as equals. In this union *you* will choose external influences that are joyous and life-affirming. One of the most important external influences is positive community.

I count my fellow musicians among my greatest allies. I remember having a crisis before a concert at the Smithsonian with master bansuri player Deepak Ram. As I paced and wrung my hands, he quietly smiled at me and said, "When I play a concert, I can't wait. It's like I'm going to a party." Right there he diffused my drama, reminding me of the real reason I play: to commune via spirit. When he practices music with others, tombak master Pezhham Akhavass doesn't call it rehearsing but rather "finding each other." We meet each other on the spiritual plane, whatever that mysterious force means to you. Thanks to kora player Daniel Berkman, I came to understand the real power of groove: accessing source through trance, giving free rein to what wants to come through. Pianist Bryan Seet (beloved partner of your author!) reflects on his standing engagement at the Alley, founded 1933 in Oakland, California: "A piano bar, at its best, is all about community. It's a congregation that meets within a space like a sanctuary, a sacred space. As a congregation, we

> It is now time in our journey together to reintegrate the external, this time from a place of internal strength.

sing and play music for the joy of it, to uplift and to connect with each other. It's a place where one can transcend our day-to-day lives and be part of something safe and comforting."

BRIGHT WAY ACTIVITY (OR IS IT A BREAK?)
Live Events

One of the best ways to cultivate community is to attend live events that interest you. You meet people with similar interests and have something to talk about right away. You get inspiration as well! Search your local community for concerts, book readings, craft circles, gardening gatherings that spark your interest: the list is endless. Look online, ask in shops that cater to your art, notice flyers. Keep an eye out everywhere for signs — they'll be revealed. Go out and support someone, just as others support you. By paying it forward, you give *and* receive the gift.

These days it's easier than ever to get cut off from direct experience, living through screens and surviving on anonymous package deliveries. While these modern amenities offer convenience and diversion, they can also chip away at our souls. Our heads may think everything is fine, but our souls know something is wrong. Terribly wrong. Community is our best antidote to this. Community restores direct experience in all its messy brilliance, fun, excitement, frustration, and challenge. Community helps us know we are alive. It mirrors who we are, for better and worse, showing us how to evolve. Community is necessary and natural. Let's call on nature once again for inspiration.

BRIGHT WAY ACTIVITY
Follow the Animals

Our cousins in the animal kingdom teach us a lot about community. Elephants have elaborate burial rituals for grieving their dead. Male emperor penguins support their mates by watching over unhatched eggs for four long and freezing months. Dolphins protect one another from shark attacks. Choose your favorite animal and research how it practices community. How can you cultivate community by following their example?

Now let's hear from a human community, this time from Bright Knowledge Harp Circle (BKHC) members. In the BKHC, members learn the Bright Way System and practice together via multiple levels of engagement through prerecorded trainings; live monthly Q&As; weekly open-house hours; the "Harp Buddy" program, which pairs members with complementary intentions; and an online forum. What does positive creative community look like? Member Janet tells us, "It challenges our limiting ideas about ourselves and our abilities, helps us share knowledge and resources, inspires us with new options and possibilities, celebrates our successes with us, and (virtually) holds our hands and wipes our tears as we grieve and mourn our losses. Having this kind of community has moved my harping and life forward far beyond what harp lessons and all the scale and arpeggio exercises in the world ever could."

BRIGHT WAY ACTIVITY
Share Your Work

Another fruitful way to cultivate community is to share your creative work. By sharing your work, you give others the opportunity to know and understand it and therefore to know and understand you. Share some of your work — a quick photo of your latest painting in progress? a draft of your latest story? — with your community now. You could invite someone over to enjoy your delicious cooking, volunteer your skills at a community garden, or set up an arts salon evening in your home. Whatever you choose to share, emphasize that you're coming from the spirit of community. You're offering a space for sharing, not providing a forum for judgment or competition.

Amazing things have emerged from these types of open-ended gatherings — entire art movements, the Slow Food movement, even community-created murals. Take a moment now to share some of your creative energy with your community, starting with something tiny, playful, and doable. You'll brighten their day!

BRIGHT WAY BREAK
Friendship

Read these words by Epicurus and allow them to wash over you. Here the word *friendship* can refer to any connection: a person, an animal, nature, or your relationship with spirit: "Of all the means which wisdom acquires to ensure happiness throughout the whole of life, by far the most important is friendship."

What Fulfillment Is Not

We've explored in depth what fulfillment is; now let's talk about what it isn't. It's not all roses and sunshine. It does not deny the darkness. *Fulfillment is not about denying your real feelings.* Pain exists. Suffering is real. It's normal to have bad days or even longer rough patches.

Pain is not our enemy. Suffering is unavoidable, yet let's not get trapped in it. Let's transmute it into something that could even be called beautiful. By expressing your suffering — for example, by engaging community — you allow others to relate to you, assist you, and feel less alone themselves. I came to understand the real power of community by witnessing firsthand the rapid and deep healing that occurs when people feel safe enough to share their pain. Connection can be reestablished through pain and suffering. Suffering can be a catalyst for change, even inspiration. Pain can point us toward better ways, more fruitful creation, deeper honesty with ourselves and others. Pain and suffering are unavoidably part of the creative experience. Why? Because they are part of human life, and creativity reflects life.

Denying pain is akin to fighting performance anxiety. Performance energy is positive when we recognize and manage it. If we try to crush it, it balloons into anxiety. Similarly, denying pain strangely increases its power, twisting it into monstrous levels of strength. Like performance energy, pain is not our opponent. *Fear is.* And as we've learned on our journey, the root of most fear is disconnection. Community and spirit now step forward as our great connectors, banishing the pain of disconnection and returning us to love.

Why Connection Is Essential to High Creativity

Without the collaboration of community and spirit, our work remains mundane rather than being a marriage of heaven and earth. Have you gone to concerts where the performer played well technically but without any soul? Spirit wasn't present. At its most extreme, this kind of artistry becomes egocentric and one-dimensional.

Break out of that box and career joyously between the many dimensions that high creativity offers you. When you create in collaboration with community and spirit, your creation becomes universal and timeless. Sharing — even *performing* — becomes natural when we surrender to this reality. Being onstage, whether actually or metaphorically, finally makes sense. It's all about cocreating with your audience in Sacred Reciprocity. The day I realized this, I wanted to shout my liberation from the rooftops. At last I knew why I was onstage! The stage is a literal platform for connection. It's a platform for collaboration — not competition.

BKHC member, composer, and scientist Masayo Honjo told me: "My music playing used to be only for me and for my teachers. But not now. The source is communicating or singing through my music to me, people around me, to the Earth, and to the universe. That is how the source communicates, and it wants to do it. I am a middleman who enjoys partaking in that communication."

This is high artistry. It shines through, whether you're decorating your house, composing a new song, or having a heartfelt conversation. This is why creativity can be anything you actively engage with. Creativity, as we've experienced, isn't limited to "fine art." When you create from this place of sincerity, others sense it instantly and resonate with you. Spirit comes through unadulterated, and we are all reborn in its presence. From the performer (which could be a cook or a person in conversation) to the audience (the one eating the food or replying) and back again, Sacred Reciprocity circles and amplifies — a mystery that's hard to capture in words yet so real that we crave it.

> When the energy behind your creativity is true connection, you create magnificently; you transmit universal energy heart to heart.

Have you ever wondered about the dividing line between okay work and great work? Why does one performance move you and another leave you cold? How does creativity actually make contact with the sublime? And can this contact be deliberately cultivated anyway? Yes, and yes! The energy powering your creativity makes that difference. When you create from a place of universal connection, you channel awesomely strong power. You connect to something bigger than yourself. This is, incidentally, why you don't have to be perfect in your delivery: when the energy behind your creativity is true connection, you create magnificently. Even seemingly simple works of art can carry breathtaking impact. They transmit universal energy heart to heart.

BRIGHT WAY ACTIVITY
What Has Moved You?

Think back to an encounter you've had with this direct-transmission universal energy. Have you ever felt overwhelmed with emotion by a song, to the point where you felt almost panicked by the grandeur? Or by a painting by your child, happy tears streaming down your cheeks?

Perhaps a pithy phrase hit you right in the gut, seemingly out of nowhere, and made you want to change your life? These are all direct-transmission energy encounters.

Florence syndrome is an extreme example of what can happen in the presence of great art. A person with this syndrome may experience fainting, dizziness, a rapid heartbeat, even hallucinations in the presence of great beauty. The phenomenon is named after Florence, Italy, since there are so many powerful works of art there, and local paramedics are even trained to help all the tourists who are struck by it. This energy is real!

When have you been awed by a creation? What was happening around you? What emotions or physical sensations did the work make you feel? Some compare this experience to what it would feel like to encounter an angel or some other divine force. I've seen others experience this same type of revelation by contemplating quantum physics. The paths to this feeling are infinite. How does communing with spirit or the mystery manifest in your life? In what objects, works, or people do you perceive the divine? How do art and other manifestations of creativity offer unique and sacred ways to connect with each other? Get to know these feelings and sensations. They, too, will become your allies.

BRIGHT WAY BREAK
Connect with Your Allies

Connect with one of your allies right now. Call them, invoke them, or simply think of them as you connect across the dimensions. Feel yourself flow in Sacred Reciprocity with them. Send them love, and feel it coming back to you in a golden loop of replenishment.

Fulfillment Is Resilience

Resilience is the capacity to bounce back from adversity. As you prepare to spiral again, fulfillment assists by increasing the speed at which you recover. The creative path is active. It's unpredictable. It's not always comfortable, to say the least. There will be challenges along the way, guaranteed. How can we prepare for these hurdles so that they don't become roadblocks?

Fulfillment fills up your well of joy, increases your confidence, and orients you toward a hopeful outlook on life. *These are the foundations of resilience.* When you're feeling down or uninspired, your well of joy replenishes you. When you're dealing with a bad review or a tough customer, your purpose reminds you of the big picture. When you have hope, other people think luck is on your side.

> Fulfillment fills up your well of joy, increases your confidence, and orients you toward a hopeful outlook on life. *These are the foundations of resilience.*

If we haven't cultivated resilience, getting back up from the ground is hard, requiring us to draw on energies we simply don't have. Eventually even small challenges can feel like we're reliving Sisyphus's predicament. When you've been knocked down, it's hard to recall anything positive. So don't rely on your memory. Instead, pore over your "I Am Fulfilled" pages and feel your energy flow back to you.

Fulfillment: What Does Success Mean to You?

Creating for its own sake is a legitimate activity, so achieving excellence and finishing things are not the only options available to you. So what if you never perform that piece or finish that book? One person's success is another person's nonevent. There's no good or bad here, no judgment. Instead, it's all about owning what honestly fulfills you. You can discover this only by actively practicing fulfillment.

Understanding what fulfills you means you can live life on your terms. Celebrate your fulfillment; it reveals what success means to *you*. Further, what you discover now will inform your next go around the spiral. The more you look, the more reasons there are to celebrate fulfillment!

Looking Ahead on Our Journey: Fear of Success

It's precisely at this crossroads of success that some may want to pull back. Quit, even. Why? If we strive for success, isn't it madness to throw it all away once we finally attain it?

We fear success for many reasons, such as worrying that we'll be isolated or made the object of envy. Perhaps we'll make other people feel small, that we will be held up to unreasonable standards, have our stuff stolen, or lose control of our lives.

But is this fear of success? Or is it really fear of failure? Do we fear that by reaching a certain level of success, we open the possibility of losing it all? That if we taste winning, we won't be able to handle losing?

Fear, you are a wily foe! You try to worm your way into almost any situation.

But you, dear reader, now have the tools to identify fear and put it in its place. Mistakes? Fine! They're allies. Isolation? Not if you're connected to genuine souls in true community. Unreasonable standards? People can hold whatever standards they like; you move to your internal beat, guided by your purpose. And what about others stealing your stuff? No one can steal your creative energy. Creativity is *engagement*, and that cannot be taken. People may copy you, but no one can be you. *No one can transmit your unique energy and purpose.*

> Understanding what fulfills you means you can live life on your terms.

BRIGHT WAY ACTIVITY
Choose Love Over Fear

As a proactive measure, recall a time when you might have engaged in self-sabotage and undermined your success. Document it so that you can recognize the warning signs sooner, before they get a chance to get a foothold. Then celebrate your brave naming of them. By this very act, you choose love over fear.

BRIGHT WAY BREAK
Remain Brave

Meditate on Hildegard's words: "Be strong and brave in this shipwrecked world in all your heavy battles against injustice. Then you will shine as the 'bright star' in eternal bliss." Whatever is happening in your life and even the world at large, remember that you can create change by being a beacon of light. Stand strong, and shine far. You are a lighthouse, helping yourself and others navigate the seas of life.

New Horizons: The Great Marriage of Yourself to Yourself

Filled up with positive energy, you've replenished and fortified. Soon you'll revisit Bright Way step one: define your purpose, this time from an elevated vantage point. Depth and meaning you never saw before will be revealed to you.

New convictions and desires will rise. Your purpose will refine. Your intentions will gain focus and power. Your practicum plan will support your intentions more elegantly and easily. Your integration will spiral up like DNA. And you'll have another appointment with fulfillment to celebrate!

Let's prepare for your new spiral by adding extra potency to one of your most important tools, harmonizing with yourself. We've worked extensively with strengthening your internal self. The final alchemical operation of *coagulation* symbolizes the great marriage within ourselves. It helps us to understand that by marrying seeming opposites within, we become stronger than ever. Ask yourself these questions to assess how your internal integration — your marriage to yourself — is going:

- How has action integrated with receptivity for you? Can you switch gears, alternating between determination and surrender? Between cerebral thinking and heart-centered feeling? Between the known and unknown?

- How have your skill and magic married thus far? What specific examples do you have of working on something with both skill and magic?

- Do you have more confidence in honoring both your need to achieve *and* your need to rest? Can you recognize when your body needs rest? What replenishes your body? What does success look like for you?

- How is your collaboration between beginner's mind and your inner expert going? Can you engage in wonder *and* discernment? Are you able to entertain all possibilities while also being able to examine those possibilities with clarity?

- What emotions, sensations, and thoughts come up for you in connection to light and dark? Do you believe one is good and one is bad? Or are they two sides of the creative coin? Does darkness frighten you?

- What other opposites have you reintegrated on our journey together?

You don't have to answer these questions right away; after all, they could easily be a lifetime's work! Rather, plant seeds that will germinate over your next spin around our spiral.

Advanced Harmonization:
Connecting Internal-External: All Is One

Having reclaimed your personal power — I bow in admiration to your brave soul! — it's time to reintegrate the external into your life. To close this chapter of your creative journey, let's ensure your reentry into the "regular" world flows seamlessly.

The truth is, we care about others. We are part of a larger world. For most of us, being of service is our highest calling. Yet it can be frightening to open yourself to others. What if we lose ourselves? What if we get sucked back into fear-based living?

Remember your safety valve! Sacred Reciprocity will

> Having reclaimed your personal power, it's time to reintegrate the external into your life.

steer you true. Remember your path: the Bright Way. You know your purpose. You know your heart. You've been around the spiral, and you're ready for this.

So now it's time to fortify one of our mightiest tools, harmonizing with yourself, with two additional stages. Review page 97 for our first iteration of harmonizing with yourself, which in summary was:

FOCUS

↓

CONNECT

↓

BREATHE

↓

OPEN

↓

EMBODY

Figure 16. The Stages of Harmonizing with Yourself

We now complete the loop with our two new stages:

1. Focus
2. Connect
3. Breathe
4. Find your center — New!
5. Open
6. Embody
7. Connect and cycle — New!

Find Your Center

I've saved discussing your center until now, because much of what we have done was focused on strengthening your core power and will. You are now ready to engage your center directly.

Your center is your primary energy locus, residing about halfway between your heart and your belly, somewhere between your solar and sacral chakras, if you're familiar with those. Everyone's center is in a slightly different place, so it may take a little while to find yours. You may experience it as your center of gravity. Sometimes people identify it as the *dan tien*, from qigong. It feels like a warm ball of energy, perhaps a flame, a personal internal battery that powers you with will and love. Will and love, because you work within Sacred Reciprocity. (Sometimes we may fear our will and what it can drive us to desire or do. Call on Sacred Reciprocity so that your will can be tempered with love.)

If you're not sure where your center is, try these techniques:

- Put your left hand flat over your navel. Sense the energy pulsing, pushing outward, radiating forth. If you don't feel it yet, move your hand around in search of that energy hot spot until you find it.

- When I was a child, I loved hula-hooping. Funnily enough, this is a great way to find your center! If you happen to have a Hula-Hoop handy, go ahead, start hooping. As you get into flow with it, you will start to perceive your center.

- You can also find your center through belly dance, another love of mine (hello cross-training!). Circle your hips in a wide arc, and picture a little ball of gold right at the center of your core, at about the level of your navel. *Important: you might feel it at your navel, or it could be a little higher or lower than that — everyone is different!* Circle around that ball. Now start making your circles smaller, zooming in on your little ball. Keep getting closer and closer to your gold — that's your center.

Since this is a physical process, it's hard to describe in words! Take a tai chi class, attend a meditation session, ask someone whose rock-solid presence you admire how they feel. Search online for centering descriptions. Again, direct experience is key. Feel free to reach out to community about finding your center. Help is one connection away!

Connect and Cycle

Sense your body-mind-spirit connecting. Just as the steps and essential elements have integrated for you, so your body-mind-spirit conjoins. Circulate this connected energy in a loop up your back and then down the front of your body. Keep this loop flowing. You might sense this energy as golden light cycling around you in a beautiful circle. Or you might perceive it as a refreshing wave of water. You might feel there's a ring of electricity crackling with dynamism around you. Whatever shows up for you is right.

Breathe in to draw the energy up your back. Breathe out to draw the energy down your front. Keep cycling and enjoying the sensations this practice brings. You might also like to follow the movement of the circle with your arms. If you practice qigong, this will look very familiar to you.

Here is the entire advanced harmonizing with yourself process, with "find your center" and "connect and cycle" included. And yes, it turns out that this is a circle as well!

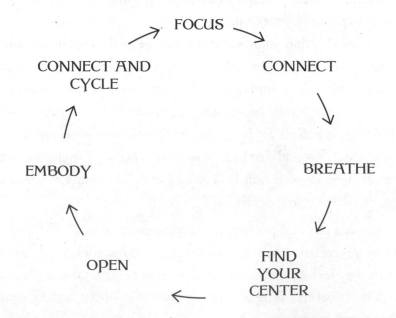

Figure 17. The Stages of Advanced Harmonizing with Yourself

As this wheel turns, you might sense your energy increasing. Feel the connection within your whole being as well as your connection with your environment. Perhaps your loop widens to embrace your instrument, your writing desk, your easel, your garden, your kitchen, your collaborator, your community.

This world is indeed a living being endowed with a soul and intelligence . . .
a single visible living entity containing all other living entities,
which by their nature are all related.

— PLATO

As time goes on, you'll be able to increase this loop of relatedness to almost infinite capacity. When I use this loop with my harp during practice, I perceive the bond between us, and practice flows more easily. When I loop with my audience, I sense us cocreating together rather than me just performing "at" them. And even when I teach large-scale gatherings online, I loop with what feels like the whole world, all of us cycling and creating together in harmony.

For now, start with what feels safe and comfortable to you, knowing it will grow with time, as all skills do.

Mysteriously, in the holiest sense of the word, the separation between the internal and the external worlds begins to blur. You recognize the sacred oneness, the inter-being of everything. As the Bhagavad Gita says, "Curving back within myself, I create again and again." The loop closes and spins with life. Light and dark marry. Action and receptivity fuel each other. Skill and magic are two ends of the same creativity pole. You and I are the same. Your story is my story. As Above, So Below.

From this place of Oneness — *the Great Work that is connection, our ultimate goal in creativity* — you are now ready to meet step one again. Now in the knowledge of what that One truly is.

Slainte, Bright One!

PART THREE

Homecoming

Valediction:
Your Creativity Spirals
Ever Outward

The Wheel Turns

Thank you for taking this courageous journey with me. It has been my honor to walk with you.

You are now an initiated Bright Way adept, a purveyor of joy and resilience who draws on the wisdom of the past and the illumination of the present to grow and inspire.

My hope now is that you go forth and share your magic in our world. Do it with conviction and confidence. Be courageous. We need you. We need your unique purpose to uplift us. You, *you*, are playing your part in helping us to evolve.

Whether you engage in creativity from the privacy of your living room or from the largest of public stages, know that your energy radiates out. It matters, literally.

As your creativity spirals ever upward, your message continually gains clarity, momentum, and beauty. Your flame burns ever brighter, illuminating your life and the lives of all who come into contact with you. Our ally throughout our journey, Hildegard of Bingen, urges us forward: "The Word is living, being, spirit, all verdant greening, all creativity. This Word manifests itself in every creature....Good people, most royal greening verdancy, rooted in the sun, you shine with radiant light."

When you reconnect to your true self through your creativity, you confirm your existence. "Know thyself" is no longer simply a saying to you; it's the pithy secret to finding meaning in life passed down through the ages, understood even before being engraved at Delphi's Temple of Apollo thousands of years ago.

You are a modern bearer of the Bright Knowledge, shining your healing message throughout our world. It is your turn to marry arts, healing, and light into your mission, as sunny Apollo did. You've mastered the ability to know thyself. Now inspire others to do the same, whether intimately from your home or from the largest platform. Remember:

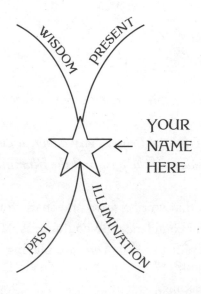

The Bright Way Charge

On the Bright Way, we believe that when we live as our true selves, we live from a place of good.

We have faith in humanity, even though we sometimes forget ourselves and act out of fear rather than love.

On the Bright Way, we believe that creativity is one of the supreme ways to reconnect to our true selves and that creativity is accessible to all.

Creativity means actively engaging with life, which can happen at any time, any place, and any age.

On the Bright Way, we know creativity manifests most strongly when we marry practical skill and intuitive magic.

Skill and magic are not predetermined at birth; they can be deliberately cultivated.

On the Bright Way, we believe creativity, safeguarded through Sacred Reciprocity, is love made manifest.

Love makes us whole again, healing us individually and globally, from the inside out.

BRIGHT WAY ACTIVITY
Your Journey

Take a moment to write down some of your reflections about your first pass around the Bright Way Spiral. Where were you when we started? Where are you now? What has surprised you about our journey? What have you let go of? What have you gained? How have you changed? How are you the same?

*You must go on a long journey before you can
really find out how wonderful home is.*

— TOVE JANSSON, *Comet in Moominland*

You Are the Star

I've shared with you how the Bright Way has taught me that darkness is not to be avoided. Darkness, in all its fertile, receptive mystery, is the great unknown. And from this vast unknown, all potential comes into being.

As a Bright Way adept, you illuminate the dark in order to partake of its richness. You embrace the unknown and make it known. You lead us to the next unknown, and you teach us to know it. This is the creative path. This is the path of connection. This is the path of love.

Look at our entire Bright Way Spiral. Notice the star in the middle. *You* are this star. You have brought together all the steps and elements of this spiral and are now ready to shine bright.

Figure 18. The Central Star

BRIGHT WAY ACTIVITY
Draw the Star

Draw the star above in your Bright Way Diary. Put your name inside it, if that feels right. How do you feel, knowing that the star is *you*?

✷ ✷ ✷

Stepping into the Unknown

You have completed one turn of the spiral. And now you get to traverse another turn of the spiral, a journey as yet unwritten. You are the star lighting the way to your own new story. As you step into the unknown as you so bravely did before, keep being your best teacher. Keep embodying that gloriously paradoxical combination of beginner's mind innocence and seasoned practitioner's expertise. Expect and welcome change as you spiral again; your experience *will* be different this time. They say the most characteristic trait of creative people is being open to change. You have grown, you have changed: the spiral widens in radiant splendor to accommodate you. Trust yourself and this journey. Trust yourself enough to hold this folk wisdom: the more you know, the more you realize you don't know.

You can now face the dark and illuminate it. You now know the opponent to life is not darkness. The opponent to life is fear, which is ultimately disconnection. As a Bright Way adept, you are a web weaver, a connector of the highest order. You're a builder of resilience, a cultivator of joy, and in possession of the ultimate guiding light: your sacred purpose. Light the way forward!

BRIGHT WAY ACTIVITY
Stay Receptive

Create a note encouraging yourself to stay open and available for your next cycle around our wheel. In your Bright Way Diary, review your list of fulfillments and write something like: "I feel happy/proud/satisfied with [insert your fulfillment here], which I accomplished because I stayed open-hearted and engaged. I commit to maintaining the joy of beginner's mind and the discernment of a growth mentality going forward."

Once we've been through a process like the Bright Way, it can be tempting to feel that we already know what to expect. Step away from the "I already know that" stance. Instead, what specific tools and perspectives can you use to stay receptive and fresh for your new horizons?

Besides beginner's mind, examples could include presence and deep listening. Flip through this book and note what pops out at you. Put these on your note and refer to your note weekly (or whenever suits you best) as a perspective booster.

Assessing Your Momentum

On the Bright Way, we understand that, as with nature, creativity flourishes in cycles. Notice your state right now. Are you energized to forge ahead and start another spiral, or do you need to rest and reflect first? Either option is fine; one is not better than the other. Remember the field lying fallow that we talked about? When we let the field be, it has a chance to replenish and become rich again. It's the same for us.

Look inside and honestly appraise where your energy is. To do this, harmonize with yourself, with the intention of finding your best course of action. Ask yourself, "Am I ready to take another turn of the spiral right now?" Pay particular attention to how your body feels. Our minds often want to plow ahead in enthusiasm; trust the body's wisdom on this one.

If you feel that you're ready to spiral again — hallmarks of being ready are feeling relaxed yet energized — review "The Bright Way Philosophy" on page 45 before taking step one again. I assure you you'll notice many things you didn't the first time!

If, on the other hand, you find you need rest or more time before you'll be ready to move ahead, review the replenishing tools you gathered during your Bright Way Breaks. Bask within those refreshing thoughts and actions. As with all cycles, after some time you'll naturally want to shift states from stillness into action, so don't worry that you'll end up on permanent break mode. Trust yourself, and keep your purpose front and center. You *will* desire to cycle back into action when the time is right.

The voice of the waves was now mixed with strange sounds;
laughter, running feet and the clanging of great bells far out to sea.

Snufkin lay still and listened. Dreaming and remembering his trip round the world. Soon I must set out again, he thought. But not yet.

— TOVE JANSSON, *Finn Family Moomintroll*

BRIGHT WAY ACTIVITY
Cultivate Your Garden

For our final activity for this turn of the spiral, buy a plant, or tend one you already have. Pick a plant that has special meaning to you, or find out the meaning of your current plants. Herbs are particularly apropos for this activity. Besides their symbolic power, you can also cook and even create scents from them. I've always been enchanted that in Celtic mythology the rowan tree is the Tree of Life and represents courage, wisdom, and protection, all major themes on our Bright Way. This feels like a thumbs-up from the universe that I am on the right path. Whatever type of plant you pick, root it with the intention of growing strong together, growth being the very foundation of creativity, as we learned earlier with the root word *ker*. Observe your plant blossom as you also bloom on your next turn around our spiral.

We Are the Bright Way: Sacred Reciprocity

In the distant past, we lived with a collective mentality, in which the individual's needs were subjugated to the group's. Over time, we threw off this restriction, and individualism rose. Today we've gotten to the point where extreme individualism has obliterated many people's sense of connection, and disconnection haunts them.

Now is our sea-change opportunity to connect the strong individual — you! — with supportive community — us! — to create a new paradigm of being. The Bright Way provides one path to this new vision.

It is my honor to be a fellow pilgrim with you on this quest. Let's carry this message of hope out into the world. Can you imagine a world in which we all feel empowered to live our creativity out loud and to shine our true selves? We can do this! Cultural anthropologist Margaret Mead fortifies us: "All social movements are founded by, guided by, motivated and seen through by the passion of individuals."

We know only 5 percent of our universe — the rest is dark energy and matter. And likewise for you: as a microcosm of the great cosmos, you hold the unknown within you. You are made of unlimited possibility longing to emerge. Connect to the unknown with your heart and imagination: you will create new universes.

> You are made of unlimited possibility longing to emerge. Connect to the unknown with your heart and imagination: you will create new universes.

Shine your light on the darkness with curiosity and wonder, and a new consciousness illuminates. You now know, heart and soul, that light and dark flow along the same spectrum, each making the other possible. If we fear darkness, we fear most of the very existence we belong to. We have nothing to fear. We recognize connection. We choose love.

This is our Bright Way.

And when you stumble in times of hopelessness, call on the Bright Way. Rely on the timeless wisdom of the sages. Honor your direct experience. Know that your fellow Bright Way practitioners are here by your side, holding hands with you across the dimensions. *Shine your light!*

By the air that is your clear sight,
By the fire of your bright spirit,
By the waters of your boundless creativity,
By the earth that is your knowing body,
May love
Be ever in your heart.
The spiral is open yet unbroken.

We are the keepers of this wisdom,
We are the keepers of this love,
We are the keepers of this courage,
We are the keepers of this strength.
May the Bright Way
Shine ever in our hearts
As our spirals intertwine ever outward.

Merry meet,
Merry part,
And merry meet again!

Acknowledgments

Just as the Bright Way is a confluence of mighty sources, so this book is the result of many rivers converging into an ocean of creativity.

My heartfelt thanks to Claudia Riemer Boutote, who set this whole journey in motion by suggesting I write a book about the Bright Way. You have been with me every step of this path. From guiding me in finding my writing voice to helping me share the Bright Way vision with the world, you have sculpted this experience to be one of love and joy.

Vladimir Baltić, your artistic vision is integral to this book. Your beautiful graphics are as useful and educational as they are lovely. Thank you for translating my napkin scribblings into the pictures of elegance presented here, and for your unending patience. Your combination of philosophical chops, artistic sensibilities, and tech know-how makes you one of a kind, Lionheart.

Thank you to Munro Magruder and Marc Allen for accepting *The Bright Way* into New World Library's impressive catalog. You are my dream publishing house, and I'm honored to be working with you.

Deep gratitude to my editors:

Georgia Hughes, who recognized the potential of *The Bright Way* and took a risk on this first-time author. Your faith fueled me!

Dave Mahony, storyteller extraordinaire. Your ability to get to the core and then craft a narrative arc around it has been so important to the evolution of this book. To spreading the wiggle.

Teresa Baily, for your deep insight into the Bright Way spirit and practice.

Your generous sharing of your expertise and your thorough, loving analysis of this book as it progressed brought it to a whole new level.

Janet Hince, for your wry eye, giant heart, and poetic sensibilities — I felt you holding my hand across the miles, reminding me always of my Purpose. Your close reading of many book drafts deepened the work and spurred me on.

Aubrey Forest, for your devotion to the Hermetic arts and your generosity in teaching the brighter way. Humor + high Hermeticism — you're an inspiring soul!

To Jessica Hatch, your early readings of this manuscript kept it on a path of clarity and relevance to the here and now. Thank you for your diligence and imagination. You started me out on the right foot, giving me energy and confidence for the whole journey ahead.

To Nirmala Nataraj, for your bridging of academia and mysticism and urging me to "stay radical." Courage is always the way.

Mimi Kusch, for your razor-sharp editing of the near-to-final manuscript. Your insightful comments brought on a slew of improvements and I can't imagine this book without them.

Bryan Seet, for your focus on the big picture and making sure this book is as inclusive as possible. Everyone can be creative, as you believe and encourage every day. (Also, thanks for lovingly putting up with the crazy writing hours.)

Kristen Cashman, for your gorgeous design sensibilities combined with copy feedback that made this book both stronger and more beautiful. You facilitated this book becoming a feast for both senses and soul.

Bon Singer, for your astute proofing combined with exuberant cheerleading. And for inspiring me to take up harp in the first place! You changed my life forever for the better.

Last and certainly not least in this amazing lineup of editors, thank you to Emily Butler, for coming in at the eleventh hour (in customary divine timing) and suggesting pivotal edits that brought powerful additional resonance to this book. Creative alchemy in the highest.

And speaking of alchemy, gratitude to Trismegista (Tristy) Taylor for amplifying the Bright Way message to the world. Your glorious name says it all!

Tracy Cunningham, you and your art department created a cover that thrills me every time I see it. The layers of meaning you captured in it are simply brilliant. I heard "expect to be 75 percent happy with the cover" from some authors. I'm over the moon 100 percent with mine!

To the practitioners of the Bright Way whose experience permeates every page of this book: thank you, Harp Ecosystem sisters and Bright Knowledge Harp Circle members. You have taught me — and continue to teach me — so much. We are Sacred Reciprocity in action.

To Francisca Santibanez, for first introducing me to the concept of Sacred Reciprocity. This was the missing link for me! Thank you for giving me this most crucial piece of the puzzle.

To my father, John Rowan, and to Colm Ó Riain, for Irish language consultation. To imbas and fios feasa!

To my ever-loving soul friends, whose constant enthusiasm and patience with my long absences is noted with gratitude: Becky Boblak, Keith Rowland, Jennifer Paulino, Christina Sarver, my Chimera musical soulmates (Moses, Sarah Jo, and Katie), many others already mentioned, and some who prefer to remain anonymous — you are all part of this creation. Now for cheers time!

I dedicate this book to my parents, Phyllis and John Rowan. Thank you for never once asking whether I considered being a musician a risky proposition, and for holding creativity (of all sorts) as the highest human endeavor. You made me who I am today. This book is a testament to how you raised me and all my dear siblings: with the convictions that limits are mirages and creativity is the greatest fulfillment in life.

Practices

Primary Bright Way Practices

Bright Way Activities

Bright Way Breaks

Illustrations

Notes

As Above, So Below

p. 5   *"Like billowing clouds"*: Gabriele Uhlein, ed., *Meditations with Hildegard of Bingen* (Rochester, VT: Bear & Company, 1983).

p. 10   *We've learned from physics*: "Newton's Three Laws of Motion," https://ccrma.stanford.edu/~jos/pasp/Newton_s_Three_Laws_Motion.html.

p. 11   *Astounding breakthroughs can happen*: Michael Ruff, "Mind Really Does Matter! An Interview with Dr. Candace Pert by Mitch Rustad," author website, October 14, 2014, http://candacepert.com/news/candace-pert-mind-body-connection.

Your Story Is My Story

p. 19   *We're discovering more and more*: As exemplified by the HeartMath Institute's research, available at https://www.heartmath.org/research.

p. 19   *This was clearly understood in the past*: Wikipedia, s.v. "Cardiocentric hypothesis," last modified October 15, 2019, https://en.wikipedia.org/wiki/Cardiocentric_hypothesis.

p. 23   *Buddhism takes this perspective*: Christoph von Fürer-Haimendorf, "The Sense of Sin in Cross-Cultural Perspective," *Man*, n.s., 9, no. 4 (1974): 550.

p. 23   *Finally, you don't have to have*: "Definition of Humanism," American Humanist Association, 2019, https://americanhumanist.org/what-is-humanism/definition-of-humanism.

p. 24   *Using the Five Love Languages*: Gary Chapman, *The Five Love Languages: The Secret to Love That Lasts* (Chicago: Northfield Publishing, 1992).

The Bright Way Readiness Quiz

p. 38   *"Dare to declare"*: Hildegard of Bingen, *Hildegard of Bingen's Book of Divine Works: With Letters and Songs*, ed. Matthew Fox (Rochester, VT: Bear & Company, 1987).

The Bright Way Revelation

p. 44   *Rudyard Kipling, author*: Arthur Gordon, "Interview with an Immortal," *Reader's Digest* (1935), reprinted as "Six Hours with Rudyard Kipling" in *Kipling Journal* (1967).

p. 44   *"Humanity, take a good look"*: From "Causae et Curae," a medieval text attributed to Hildegard of Bingen, https://healthyhildegard.com/causae-et-curae; and quoted in *Hildegard of Bingen: On Natural Philosophy and Medicine*, trans. Margret Berger (Rochester, NY: D. S. Brewer, 1999).

The Bright Way Philosophy

p. 45   *"a great treasury of learning"*: Caitlín Matthews and John Matthews, *The Encyclopedia of Celtic Myth and Legend: A Definitive Sourcebook of Magic, Vision, and Lore* (Guilford, CT: Lyons Press, 2004), 1.

p. 50   *"Love is born into every human being"*: Plato, *The Symposium and the Phaedrus: Plato's Erotic Dialogues*, trans. William S. Cobb (Albany: State Univ. of New York Press, 1993).

p. 52   *Father of modern physics*: Isaac Newton, *Quaestiones Quaedam Philosophiae* [*Certain Philosophical Questions*] (1664), http://www.newtonproject.ox.ac.uk/view/texts/normalized/THEM00092.

p. 53   *As pioneering seventeenth-century*: Wikipedia, s.v. *"Pensées"* ("Thoughts") [by Blaise Pascal], last modified June 1, 2019, https://en.wikipedia.org/wiki/Pens%C3%A9es.

p. 53   *Quite the opposite*: Theodor Reik, *Listening with the Third Ear: The Inner Experience of a Psychoanalyst* (New York: Farrar, Straus and Giroux, 1948), vii.

The Bright Way Spiral

p. 64   *"You have seen what happens"*: Nikos Kazantzakis, *Zorba the Greek* (London: Faber and Faber, 1961; repr., 1987), 188.

p. 75   *"Glance at the sun"*: Matthew Fox, *Original Blessing: A Primer in Creation Spirituality Presented in Four Paths, Twenty-Six Themes, and Two Questions* (New York: TarcherPerigee, 2000).

p. 76   *"Nature does nothing uselessly"*: P. M. Dunn, "Aristotle (384–322 BC): Philosopher and Scientist of Ancient Greece," *Archives of Disease in Childhood: Fetal and Neonatal Edition* 91, no. 1 (2006): F75–77 https://www.ncbi.nlm.nih.gov/pmc /articles/PMC2672651.

Step One: Define Your Purpose

p. 82   *"We humans, alone of all the animals"*: Jim Gasperini, "Fire in the Mind: How We Imagined Fire, from the Burning Bush to Burning Man" (unpublished manuscript).

p. 84   *"We have all a better guide in ourselves"*: Jane Austen, *Mansfield Park* (1814; Project Gutenberg, 2010), chap. 42, https://www.gutenberg.org/files/141/141-h /141-h.htm#link2HCH0042.

p. 86   *"The beginning in every task"*: Plato, *The Republic*, trans. Benjamin Jowett (New York: Vintage Classics, 1991).

p. 87   *Aristotle understood the power*: Wikiquote, s.v. "Aristotle," last modified August 25, 2019, https://en.wikiquote.org/wiki/Aristotle.

p. 87   *"happiness is the ultimate end"*: "Aristotle," The Pursuit of Happiness (website), https://www.pursuit-of-happiness.org/history-of-happiness/aristotle.

p. 88   *Shinichi Suzuki, whose Suzuki Method*: "Shinichi Suzuki," obituary, *The Economist*, February 5, 1998, https://www.economist.com/obituary/1998/02/05 /shinichi-suzuki.

p. 88   *"Where the love is deep"*: "Shinichi Suzuki."

p. 88   *Suzuki, who mostly worked with children*: "Shinichi Suzuki."

p. 90   *As far back as imperial Rome*: Marcus Aurelius, *The Meditations of Marcus Aurelius*, trans. George Long (Mount Vernon, NY: Peter Pauper Press, 1942), 5:16.

p. 91   *On this journey you are cycling*: Thich Nhat Hanh, *Interbeing: Fourteen Guidelines for Engaged Buddhism* (Berkeley, CA: Parallax Press, rev. ed., 1987).

p. 93   *This idea was furthered*: B. J. Fogg, Tiny Habits (website), https://www.tiny habits.com.

p. 101   *We're born with synesthesia*: Daphne Maurer, Laura C. Gibson, and Ferrinne Spector, "Synesthesia in Infants and Very Young Children," in *The Oxford Handbook of Synesthesia*, ed. Julia Simner and Edward Hubbard (Oxford: Oxford Univ. Press, 2013), https://www.oxfordhandbooks.com/view/10.1093/oxfordhb /9780199603329.001.0001/oxfordhb-9780199603329-e-003.

Step Two: Set Your Intentions

p. 112   *The eighty-twenty rule shows*: Wikipedia, s.v. "Pareto principle," last modified October 4, 2019, https://en.wikipedia.org/wiki/Pareto_principle.

p. 113   *It's a strange phenomenon that*: "Babies and Phoneme Filtering," Voxy, May 10, 2012, https://voxy.com/blog/ 2012/05/babies-phoneme-filtering.

p. 116   *On the Bright Way, you are encouraged*: Shunryu Suzuki, *Zen Mind, Beginner's Mind* (Boston: Shambhala, 2006), 2.

p. 121   *Candace Pert observes*: Candace Pert, *Your Body Is Your Subconscious Mind*, read by the author (Louisville, CO: Sounds True; unabridged ed., 2004), audiobook.

p. 125   *"Life is an unfoldment"*: "Hypatia," *The Literature Network*, http://www.online -literature.com/elbert-hubbard/journeys-vol-ten/10.

p. 128   *Your story is being told*: Martha C. Nussbaum, "How to Write about Poverty," *Times Literary Supplement*, October 10, 2012.

Step Three: Create Your Practicum Plan

p. 133   *"Those who know, do"*: Lee S. Shulman, "Those Who Understand: Knowledge Growth in Teaching," *Educational Researcher* 15, no. 2 (Feb. 1986): 14.

p. 142   *We're motivated by emotion*: J. R. Blackburn, A. G. Phillips, A. Jakubovic, and H. C. Fibiger, "Dopamine and Preparatory Behavior: II. A Neurochemical Analysis," *Behavioral Neuroscience* 103, no. 1 (Feb. 1989): 15–23, https://www .ncbi.nlm.nih.gov/pubmed/2923667.

p. 144   *"Research suggests that taking one day"*: Aaron Edelheit, *The Hard Break: The Case for the 24/6 Lifestyle* (Washington, DC: Ideapress Publishing, 2018).

p. 146   *"Daily struggles we know"*: Daniel Ladinsky, ed. and trans., *Love Poems from God: Twelve Sacred Voices from the East and West* (New York: Penguin, 2002), 184.

p. 148   *Do this right after practice*: Daniel Coyle, *The Talent Code* (New York: Bantam, 2009).

p. 149   *Two thousand years ago*: Plato. *Plato's The Republic*, trans. Benjamin Jowett (New York Books, 1943), bk. 7.

p. 149   *Incredibly, given the amount*: G. A. Miller, "The Magical Number Seven, Plus or Minus Two: Some Limits on Our Capacity for Processing Information," *Psychological Review* 63, no. 2 (1956): 81–97.

p. 149   *Short-term memory is where*: Yana Weinstein, "How Long Is Short-Term Memory? Shorter Than You Might Think," *The Learning Scientists*, April 13, 2017, http://www.learningscientists.org/blog/2017/4/13-1.

p. 153   *There's even evidence that mistakes*: "Mistakes Grow Your Brain," YouCubed, https://www.youcubed.org/evidence/mistakes-grow-brain; "The Power of Making Mistakes," YoungMathematicians.edc, http://youngmathematicians.edc .org/mindset/the-power-of-making-mistakes.

Step Four: Integration

p. 162   *Education pioneer Maria Montessori*: Maria Montessori, *The Advanced Montessori Method: The Montessori Elementary Material*, trans. Arthur Livingston (New York: Frederick A. Stokes, 1917), 309.

p. 163   *"Underneath all the texts"*: As quoted in Susan Gillingham, *Psalms through the Centuries*, vol. 1 (Hoboken, NJ: Wiley-Blackwell, 2012).

p. 169   *"There is one thing that when cultivated"*: The Numerical Discourses of the Buddha: A Complete Translation of the Anguttara Nikaya (The Teachings of the Buddha), annotated edition, trans. Bhikkhu Bodhi (Somerville, MA: Wisdom Publications, 2012), passage 1:43.

p. 171   *Your body is an ongoing creative work*: Simone de Beauvoir, *The Second Sex*. (1949; repr., New York: Vintage, 2011), 68.

p. 175   *Recall that you have a split second*: Daniel Coyle, *The Talent Code* (New York: Bantam, 2009).

p. 176   *Everything is grist*: As quoted by Rodin's student Malvina Hoffman in her book *Heads and Tales* (New York: Charles Scribner's Sons, 1936), 47.

p. 185   *As Thich Nhat Hanh reminds us*: Thich Nhat Hanh, *No Mud, No Lotus: The Art of Transforming Suffering* (Berkeley, CA: Parallax, 2014).

p. 188   *As Aristotle wrote*: Aristotle, *Aristotle's Nicomachean Ethics*, trans. Robert C. Bartlett and Susan D. Collins (Chicago: Univ. of Chicago Press, 2012), 14.

p. 189   *All the research is in*: Ferris Jabr, "Why Your Brain Needs More Downtime," *Scientific American*, October 15, 2013, https://www.scientificamerican.com/article /mental-downtime.

Step Five: Fulfillment

p. 197   *"'Come on, Zorba,' I cried"*: Nikos Kazantzakis, *Zorba the Greek* (London: Faber and Faber, 1961; repr., 1987), 293.

p. 204   *"You turn the wheel"*: Kazantzakis, *Zorba*, 20.

p. 207   *We've discovered that fulfillment*: Helen Walters, "Want to Be Happy? Be Grateful: Brother David Steindl-Rast at TEDGlobal 2013," TEDBlog, June 14, 2013, https://blog.ted.com/want-to-be-happy-be-grateful-brother-david-steindl -rast-at-tedglobal-2013.

p. 208   *We "inter-are"*: Thich Nhat Hanh, *Interbeing: Fourteen Guidelines for Engaged Buddhism* (Berkeley, CA: Parallax Press, rev. ed., 1987); Thich Nhat Hanh's calligraphy of "we inter-are" is viewable at https://store.lionsroar.com/products /we-inter-are-thich-nhat-hanh?variant=10810363139.

p. 212   *"Of all the means which wisdom acquires"*: Ben Gazur, "Why Epicurus Matters Today," *The Mantle*, https://themantle.com/philosophy/why-epicurus-matters -today, accessed November 25, 2019.

p. 218   *Meditate on Hildegard's words*: Hildegard of Bingen's letter to Archbishop Philip of Cologne, as quoted in Hildegard of Bingen, *Hildegard of Bingen's Book of Divine Works: With Letters and Songs*, ed. Matthew Fox (Rochester, VT: Bear & Company, 1987).

p. 223   *"This world is indeed a living being"*: Plato, *Timaeus*, trans. Peter Kalkavage, second edition (Newburyport, MA: Focus Philosophical Library, 2016), 30b–c, 33b.

P. 223   *"Curving back within myself"*: Bhagavad Gita 9:8, quoted in Deepak Chopra, *Return of the Rishi* (1988; repr., Boston: Houghton-Mifflin, 1991), 189.

Valediction

p. 228   *Our ally throughout our journey*: Matthew Fox, *Original Blessing: A Primer in Creation Spirituality Presented in Four Paths, Twenty-Six Themes, and Two Questions* (New York: TarcherPerigee, 2000).

p. 230   *"You must go on a long journey"*: Tove Jansson, *Comet in Moominland*, trans. Elizabeth Portch (1951; repr., New York: Square Fish, 2010).

p. 231   *They say the most characteristic*: Scott Barry Kaufman and Carolyn Gregoire, *Wired to Create: Unraveling the Mysteries of the Creative Mind* (New York: TarcherPerigee, 2016).

p. 232   *"The voice of the waves"*: Tove Jansson, *Finn Family Moomintroll*, trans. Elizabeth Portch (1958; repr., New York: Square Fish, 2010).

p. 234   *Cultural anthropologist Margaret Mead*: As quoted in Michael S. Matthews and Jaime Castellano, *Talent Development for English Language Learners: Identifying and Developing Potential* (Waco, TX: Prufrock Press, 2013).

p. 234   *We know only 5 percent of our universe*: Dr. Mamta Patel Nagaraja, "Dark Energy, Dark Matter," NASA Science, last updated November 22, 2019, https://science .nasa.gov/astrophysics/focus-areas/what-is-dark-energy.

Bibliography

Aristotle. *Aristotle's Nicomachean Ethics.* Translated by Robert C. Bartlett and Susan D. Collins. Chicago: Univ. of Chicago Press, 2012.

"Aristotle: Introduction: Aristotle's Definition of Happiness," 2018. https://www.pursuit -of-happiness.org/history-of-happiness/aristotle.

Aurelius, Marcus. *The Meditations of Marcus Aurelius.* Translated by George Long. Mount Vernon, NY: Peter Pauper Press, 1942.

Austen, Jane. *Mansfield Park.* 1814; Project Gutenberg, 2010. https://www.gutenberg.org /files/141/141-h/141-h.htm#link2HCH0042.

"Babies and Phoneme Filtering." Voxy. May 10, 2012. https://voxy.com/blog/ 2012/05 /babies-phoneme-filtering.

Beauvoir, Simone de. *The Second Sex.* 1949. Reprint, New York: Vintage, 2011.

Bhagavad Gita. http://www.bhagavad-gita.org/Gita/verse-09-08.html.

Blackburn J. R., A. G. Phillips, A. Jakubovic, and H. C. Fibiger. "Dopamine and Preparatory Behavior: II. A Neurochemical Analysis." *Behavioral Neuroscience* 103, no. 1 (Feb. 1989). https://www.ncbi.nlm.nih.gov/pubmed/2923667.

Bodhi, Bhikkhu, trans. *The Numerical Discourses of the Buddha: A Complete Translation of the Anguttara Nikaya (The Teachings of the Buddha).* Annotated edition. Somerville, MA: Wisdom Publications, 2012. Passage I 43.

Chapman, Gary. *The Five Love Languages.* Chicago: Northfield Publishing, 1992.

Coyle, Daniel. *The Talent Code.* New York: Bantam, 2009.

"Definition of Humanism." American Humanist Association. 2019. https://american humanist.org/what-is-humanism/definition-of-humanism.

Dunn, P. M. "Aristotle (384–322 BC): Philosopher and Scientist of Ancient Greece." *Archives of Disease in Childhood: Fetal and Neonatal Edition* 91, no. 1 (2006): F75–77. https://www.ncbi.nlm.nih.gov/pmc/articles/PMC2672651.

Edelheit, Aaron. *The Hard Break: The Case for the 24/6 Lifestyle*. Washington, DC: Ideapress Publishing, 2018.

Fogg, B. J. Tiny Habits (website). https://www.tinyhabits.com.

Fox, Matthew. *Original Blessing: A Primer in Creation Spirituality Presented in Four Paths, Twenty-Six Themes, and Two Questions*. New York: TarcherPerigee, 2000.

Gasperini, Jim. "Fire in the Mind: How We Imagined Fire, from the Burning Bush to Burning Man." Unpublished manuscript.

Gillingham, Susan. *Psalms through the Centuries*, vol. 1. Hoboken, NJ: Wiley-Blackwell, 2012.

Gordon, Arthur. "Interview with an Immortal." *Reader's Digest* (1935). Reprinted as "Six Hours with Rudyard Kipling" in *Kipling Journal* (1967).

Hildegard of Bingen. *Hildegard of Bingen: On Natural Philosophy and Medicine*. Translated by Margret Berger. Rochester, NY: D. S. Brewer, 1999.

———. *Hildegard of Bingen's Book of Divine Works: With Letters and Songs*. Edited by Matthew Fox. Rochester, VT: Bear & Company, 1987.

Hoffman, Malvina. *Heads and Tales*. New York: Charles Scribner's Sons, 1936.

Jabr, Ferris. "Why Your Brain Needs More Downtime," *Scientific American*, October 15, 2013, https://www.scientificamerican.com/article/mental-downtime.

Jansson, Tove. *Comet in Moominland*. Translated by Elizabeth Portch. 1951. Reprint, New York: Square Fish, 2010.

———. *Finn Family Moomintroll*. Translated by Elizabeth Portch. 1958. Reprint, New York: Square Fish, April 27, 2010.

Kaufman, Scott Barry, and Carolyn Gregoire. *Wired to Create: Unraveling the Mysteries of the Creative Mind*. New York: TarcherPerigee, 2016.

Kazantzakis, Nikos. *Zorba the Greek*. London: Faber and Faber, 1961. Reprint, 1987.

Ladinsky, Daniel, ed. and trans. *Love Poems from God: Twelve Sacred Voices from the East and West*. New York: Penguin, 2002.

Langford, Joe, and Pauline Rose Clance. "The Imposter Phenomenon: Recent Research Findings Regarding Dynamics, Personality and Family Patterns and Their Implications for Treatment." *Psychotherapy* 30, no. 3 (1993): 495–501.

Matthews, Caitlín, and John Matthews. *The Encyclopedia of Celtic Myth and Legend: A Definitive Sourcebook of Magic, Vision, and Lore*. Guilford, CT: Lyons Press, 2004.

Matthews, Michael S., and Jaime Castellano. *Talent Development for English Language Learners: Identifying and Developing Potential*. Waco, TX: Prufrock Press, 2013.

Maurer, Daphne, Laura C. Gibson, and Ferrinne Spector. "Synesthesia in Infants and Very Young Children." In *The Oxford Handbook of Synesthesia*. Edited by Julia Simner and Edward Hubbard. Oxford: Oxford Univ. Press, 2013. https://www.oxfordhandbooks.com/view/10.1093/oxfordhb/9780199603329.001.0001/oxfordhb-9780199603329-e-003.

Miller, G. A. "The Magical Number Seven, Plus or Minus Two: Some Limits on Our Capacity for Processing Information." *Psychological Review* 63, no. 2 (1956): 81–97.

Montessori, Maria. *The Advanced Montessori Method: The Montessori Elementary Material.* Translated by Arthur Livingston. New York: Frederick A. Stokes, 1917.

Newton, Isaac. *Quaestiones Quaedam Philosophiae [Certain Philosophical Questions].* 1664. http://www.newtonproject.ox.ac.uk/view/texts/normalized/THEM00092.

"Newton's Three Laws of Motion." https://ccrma.stanford.edu/~jos/pasp/Newton_s _Three_Laws_Motion.html.

Nhat Hanh, Thich. *Answers from the Heart: Practical Responses to Life's Burning Questions.* Berkeley, CA: Parallax Press, 2009.

———. *Interbeing: Fourteen Guidelines for Engaged Buddhism.* Revised edition. Berkeley, CA: Parallax Press, 1987.

———. *No Mud, No Lotus: The Art of Transforming Suffering.* Berkeley, CA: Parallax Press, 2014.

Nussbaum, Martha C. "How to Write about Poverty." *Times Literary Supplement*, October 10, 2012.

Pert, Candace. *Your Body Is Your Subconscious Mind.* Audiobook read by the author. Unabridged edition. Louisville, CO: Sounds True, 2005.

Plato. *Plato's The Republic.* Translated by Benjamin Jowett. New York: New York Books, 1943.

———. *The Symposium and The Phaedrus: Plato's Erotic Dialogues.* Translated by William S. Cobb. Albany: State Univ. of New York Press, 1993.

———. *Timaeus.* Translated by Peter Kalkavage. Second edition. Newburyport, MA: Focus Philosophical Library, 2016. 30b–c, 33b.

Reik, Theodor. *Listening with the Third Ear: The Inner Experience of a Psychoanalyst.* New York: Farrar, Straus and Giroux, 1948.

Ruff, Michael. "Mind Really Does Matter! An Interview with Dr. Candace Pert by Mitch Rustad," October 14, 2014. http://candacepert.com/news/candace-pert-mind -body-connection.

"Shinichi Suzuki." Obituary. *The Economist*, February 5, 1998. https://www.economist .com/obituary/1998/02/05/shinichi-suzuki.

Shulman, Lee S. "Those Who Understand: Knowledge Growth in Teaching." *Educational Researcher* 15, no. 2 (Feb. 1986).

Suzuki, Shunryu. *Zen Mind, Beginner's Mind.* Boston: Shambhala, 2006.

Uhlein, Gabriele, ed. *Meditations with Hildegard of Bingen.* Rochester, VT: Bear & Company, 1983.

von Fürer-Haimendorf, Christoph. "The Sense of Sin in Cross-Cultural Perspective." *Man*, n.s., 9, no. 4 (1974), 539–56.

Weinstein, Yana. "How Long Is Short-Term Memory? Shorter Than You Might Think." *The Learning Scientists*, April 13, 2017. http://www.learningscientists.org/blog /2017/4/13-1.

About the Author

Diana Rowan is a creative alchemist and founder of the Bright Way Guild, a virtual learning environment dedicated to transforming and inspiring a global community of creatives. From her youngest years, the classical inquiry "What makes a good life?" has driven Diana, and sharing her hard-won discoveries with others is her mission. Having recovered from a soul-crushing case of stage fright and other challenges, Diana believes that by shining light on the darkness we fear, we can all become courageous purveyors of Bright Knowledge and live the good life.

Diana was born in Dublin, Ireland, to college-student parents, setting the stage for a lifetime of lively learning and seeking. Soon thereafter, her father became a diplomat for the Irish government, taking his family all over the world in a cosmopolitan pilgrimage. Respect for arts and cultures has always been second nature in Diana's family, along with a deep streak of mysticism, as embodied by her astrologer mother.

This unusual combination of intellectual seeking, cultural bridging, mystical opening, and artistic engagement is the hallmark of Diana's life, whether that be in composing music, teaching, writing, or choosing a wine. Diana holds an MM in classical piano performance and a PhD in music theory.

www.dianarowan.com